Valuable assistance in creating this book was rendered by the following:

A very special thanks to Harvey Fink, President of the Johnson Historical Museum and Mr. and Mrs. John Lavanchy. John is the ranch foreman and President of the Cochise County Historical Society. These three people gave the author authorization to use the guest house and access to all the research material and photographs at the ranch, museum and the Cochise County Historical Society.

Johnson Historical Museum of the Southwest
Cochise County Historical Society, Douglas
Department of Library, Archives and Public
Records, State of Arizona, Phoenix
Cochise County Library, Bisbee • Tombstone Reading Station
Tombstone Epitaph and Prospector • Southwest Stockman, Willcox
Douglas Daily Dispatch • Bisbee Daily Review
The Silver Lady, Tombstone • Arizona Historical Society, Tucson
Talei Publishers, Inc., Honolulu
Richard and Irise Lapidus Western History
Collection, Simi Valley, California
National Archives, Washington, D.C.
Jodi Hoffman • Mary Dolores
Nancy Sawyer • Louise Salinas
Linda King • Bonnie Short
John Rose • Steve and Marge Elliott
Jerry Guerich
Kevin and Beverly Mulkins
Southwest of John Slaughter by Allen Erwin,
Arthur H. Clark Company, Glendale, California
Cora Viola Slaughter Memoirs
Viola Slaughter Biographical File
Leonard Alverson, True Experiences
Slaughter File, Brophy Papers

Sheriff John Slaughter – Tombstone, Arizona

Introduction

Author's Comment:

A man, aptly named Slaughter, brought law and order to Cochise County with the law in one hand and a pearl handled .44 in the other.

It will be informative to compare John Slaughter's brand of law enforcement with what we have today. John would be totally disgusted at our efforts as are all of us who have not buried our heads in the sand. There is no doubt whatever that the liberal politicians and judges have made it absolutely impossible for anyone to enforce the law. They have also made it illegal for anyone to defend themselves or their property.

Slaughter had little time or respect for politicians, judges or juries. When they became too lenient on known criminals, he simply acted independently of them.

Gangs of criminals roam our cities' streets and crime rates have soared. Citizens are afraid to leave their homes. No effort is made to halt the riots where many of our large cities have been torched costing taxpayers billions of dollars. Looting is accepted as a God given right. Yet the pansy picking liberals want to disarm law abiding citizens so that they will be unable to protect themselves. God forbid that anyone would shoot a criminal in defense of their life or that of their family. And never, never, ever even think about the use of force to protect your property.

John Slaughter would have put enough bullet holes in such punks that they would have looked like Swiss Cheese and that would have ended all the foolishness. When John was missing cattle and caught Ike Clanton on his range, he said, "If I catch you or your kin on my range again, I'll kill you!" Ike understood and Slaughter's cattle quit disappearing. Simple solution.

Liberals prance about waving hankies and placards, shrieking that anything that goes boom or bang is evil and must be outlawed; and that national defense must be cut drastically to allow more money for social programs which have never worked and never will. They also think it would be cool to open the nation's borders to any and all who want a free ride from the cradle to the grave, at the taxpayer's expense, of course.

The first thing Sheriff Slaughter would have done in such a situation would have been to shove the placards where they would absolutely do the country the most good. And when he saw that there was no end to how far the liberals will go to illegally disarm law abiding Americans he would have said "Why don't you come and get my gun?"

When people perform criminal acts time and time again, there is no reason in keeping them around as society does today, particularly not at taxpayer expense. They have been losers all their lives and they will die losers.

Slaughter had a fine, efficient program for these repeat criminals, "Hit the trail or I will bury you!"

The end is approaching because our liberal government insists on being all things to all people.

As usual the author has made no effort to be politically or socially correct as that had not a damn thing to do with settling the west...or anything else for that matter.

CONTENTS

The San Bernardino 1

Slaughter, the Man 11

New Mexico and Viola 23

On the San Pedro 35

Sheriff of Cochise County 1887 - 1890 53

John Slaughter's Place 107

Apache May 143

Revolution 153

The Out Trail 163

THE SAN BERNARDINO

For centuries human beings have inhabited the San Bernardino Valley because of the abundance of water. Human bones have been unearthed there and dated at more than 1,000 years B.C. Bones of animals that are now extinct have been found there, too--horse, camel, mammoth, etc.

Archaeologists made a dig at the Slaughter Ranch site and unearthed a Salado settlement of four houses consisting of twenty two rooms. In these were a variety of beads, shell jewelry, arrowheads, metates, manos, scrapers, knives, bone tools, ornaments, and pottery.

The Salado people moved into the Hohokam area of south central Arizona around 1300 A.D. Shortly after, the Opatas moved north from around the Bavispe area in Sonora and began to farm in the San Bernardino.

After 1500 A.D. the abundance of water made this location a favorite stopover for the nomadic Apaches. By the time that the Spanish began to arrive, numerous Indian tribes had long known and used the area.

There is no way to determine which Europeans were the first to come into Arizona. Survivors of the Narvaez Expedition to Florida, Cabeza de Vaca and three of his men were most likely the first Europeans to see the valley. They were traveling on well defined Indian trails in 1538, as they journeyed from the gulf coast of Texas to Mexico City.

Francisco Vasques de Coronado probably traveled through the area when he led an expedition north in 1540. Fray Marcos de Niza was likely in the area while searching for the fabled "Seven Cities of Cibola" in 1540-1541.

That Jesuit priest, Eusebio Kino, who built numerous missions in what is now Arizona and Sonora, passed through this region in 1694, during his explorations. The San Bernardino Valley became the customary route for missionaries, soldiers, and settlers traveling from old Mexico to Santa Fe, New Mexico.

In 1775, Spain began to build presidios to protect the northern Sonoran frontier. The first was San Bernardino (1775-1779), then Santa Cruz de Terrenate (1776-1779), located near Tombstone on the San Pedro River, and San Augustine (17761821), in Tucson on the Santa Cruz River. All three of these presidios were eventually abandoned because of Apache attacks, isolation and serious supply problems.

Presidio San Bernardino was built approximately one mile south of where John Slaughter's house now stands. Captain Juan Bautista de Anza, founder of San Francisco had camped there in 1773. The favorable report that he wrote induced the Marquis de Rubi, a representative of Spain, to construct a presidio and maintain a garrison there as a defense against the Apaches. The mesa near San Bernardino is still called "Mesa de la Avansada" (Mesa of the Advance Guards). It was abandoned five years later because the small garrison was unable to defend itself.

In December, 1820, a Lieutenant Ignacio Perez of Arispe filed a petition for a private grant of land in the San Bernardino Valley.

In his petition, the twenty-nine year old Perez made note that the particular area was at the time depopulated and that, if he was given the grant, it would form a buffer between the rest of Sonora and the hostile Apaches.

Of course the fact that his father, Jose Perez Ortiz owned the rich mines at Cananea, and that his family was also one of the most prominent land holding families in Sonora, did not hurt his cause.

Perez had also supported the independence movement and a grateful Emperor Augustine de Iturbide repaid him by promoting him to lieutenant colonel and giving him his grant. Thus, he was permitted to "buy" the land he desired.

The new colonel bought four sitios for sixty pesos; thirty pesos for one sitio with springs, and ten pesos each for three dry sitios. He was also allowed to buy what was called "excess lands" which brought his entire holdings to approximately 100,000 acres. This enormous grant cost him ninety pesos plus fees.

Most likely Ignacio never lived on his huge land grant, but probably was a frequent visitor. He continued his military career, commanding at times the presidios of Fronteras and San Buenaventura. That he was successful is evident as when Don Martin Carrera was installed as President of Mexico in 1855, Perez was Sonora's representative at the Junta de Notables.

Rafael Elias, Perez's brother-in-law, was the man who restored the abandoned presidio and developed the ranch. It was he who paid for 4,000 head of cattle that Ignacio Perez brought from Tumacacori Mission. By 1835, the grant was stocked with 100,000 head of cattle, horses, and mules.

At the time that this land grant was made, it lay entirely within the boundaries of Mexico. It encompassed the area from the San Simon Valley watershed in the north to Pitaicachi Peak in the Sierra Madres to the south; and from the Guadalupe and Peloncillo Mountains east to the Perillas and Pedregosas to the west. This huge cattle empire, built by Ignacio Perez and Rafael Elias, did not endure very long. Relentless and persistent attacks by the Apaches drove them out completely, even forcing them to abandon the vast herd of livestock.

This ranch lay in decay for many years battered by the elements. In 1846 the "Mormon Battalion", a portion of General Stephen Kerney's "Army of the West", under command of Lt. Colonel St. George Cooke, traveled from Santa Fe to San Diego. During this journey they camped just southwest of the current ranch house.

The command was guided by the famous mountain men, Pauline Weaver, Antoine Leroux, and Baptiste Charbonneau. Their objective was to establish a wagon road to San Diego.

A few days later Cooke and his men encountered a herd of the wild descendants of the Perez-Elias cattle near where Charleston was later built. These wild cattle attacked the men and brought about the incident known as the "Battle of the Bulls". Needless to say, the battalion ate well on "wild beef' from the abandoned cattle.

Cooke's diary told of the encounter:

"At two o'clock again I came to a canon and several men having been wounded and much meat killed, I encamped, sending Charbonneau to examine the country.

"There was quite an engagement with bulls, as I had to direct the men to load their muskets to defend themselves. They attacked in some instances without provocation; one ran on a man, caught him in the thigh and threw him clear over his body lengthwise, then it charged on a team, ran his head under the first mule, tore out the entrails of the one beyond, and threw them both over. Another ran against a sergeant, who escaped with severe bruises, as the horns went on each side of him; a third ran at a horse tied to a wagon and as it escaped, its great momentum forced the hind part of the wagon from the road. I saw one rush at some pack mules and gore one so that its entrails came out broken. I also saw an immense coal black bull charge on Corporal Frost of A Company; he stood his ground, while the animal rushed right on for 100 yards. I was close by, and believed the man was in great danger of his life and spoke to him; he aimed his musket very deliberately and only fired when the beast was within ten paces and it fell headlong almost at his feet. One man, when charged on threw himself flat on the ground, and the bull jumped over him and passed on.

"I have seen the heart of a bull with two balls through it, that ran on a man with these wounds and two others through the lungs. Lt. Stoneman was accidentally wounded in the thumb.

"Today we crossed a pretty stream which I have called "Bull Run". About ten bulls were killed and butchered."

From the "Mormon Battalion's" trip emerged the first transcontinental wagon route across the Southwest. A few years later this became a favorite trail for prospectors and settlers en route to the California gold fields.

U.S. Boundary Commissioner John R. Bartlett made his camp at San Bernardino springs in 1851 and again in 1852. In his report he described the remains of the old presidio and the hacienda built by Perez-Elias:

"It was about 100 feet square, with a courtyard in the center and adjoining it were others with small apartments, the whole extending over a space of about two acres, was enclosed with a wall of high adobe, with the regular bastions for defense. Ruins, consisting of piles of adobe melt, may still be seen on the Mexican side of the border."

Although all the original grant lay in Mexico, following the Gadsden Purchase in 1853, the international border was reestablished, placing 2,383 acres in the United States and the remainder in Mexico.

The Second Boundary Commission report of 1854 stated: "Adjoining this ranch are numerous springs, spreading out into rushy ponds, and giving issue to a small stream of running water. The valley is covered with a coarse growth of grass."

San Bernardino springs were often used as the headquarters for a military base of operations when pressure was exerted on Congress to control the Apaches. Two companies of soldiers and Indian scouts from the Sixth Cavalry under Captain Daniel Madden out of Fort Grant established a supply camp at the springs in 1878. It was called Camp Supply. Such a military post only a few yards from the international border made the Mexicans extremely nervous. Two weeks after its establishment, Major C.E. Compton ordered the base moved north because of probable diplomatic difficulties with the Mexican government. Camp Supply was moved 28 miles north into the

White River Canyon in the Chiricahua Mountains on April 21, 1878. It became Camp John A. Rucker.

General Crook returned as the Commander of the Department of Arizona in 1882. After he had evaluated the situation he said:

"No military department can well have been in a more desperate plight, with more than 600 Apaches just across the border in Mexico."

On April 23, 1883. Crook set out from Willcox and established a base camp at San Bernardino Springs. Then he entered Mexico with five officers, forty-two enlisted men from the Sixth Cavalry, and 193 Indian scouts under officers Gatewood, Crawford and Mackay, with Al Sieber as Chief of Scouts, and Scouts Archie McIntosh and Sam Bowman. Mickey Free and Severiano were along as interpreters.

Crook's group disappeared into Mexico for forty two days and absolutely nothing was heard from them. then they reappeared with Apaches: five chiefs, fifty-two warriors, and 273 women and children. Afterward, stragglers kept pouring into the San Carlos Reservation until by June, 1884, Crook reported, "for the first time ever the Apaches are at peace."

In 1884 John Slaughter purchased the San Bernardino from Guillermo Andrade of Guaymas, Mexico, and the other heirs. Acquiring adjacent land and leasing more, Slaughter built a cattle empire; one of the largest cattle ranches in Arizona. His cattle grazed a quarter million acres from the Chiricahua Mountains in Arizona to the end of the Sierra Madres in Mexico.

In May 1885, Geronimo caused several Apaches to "jump" the reservation. These small bands of raiders left trails of blood and death all through southeast Arizona, southwest New Mexico, and northeast Sonora.

To show what even a very small band of Apaches could do, a war leader, called Josanie led a raiding party of ten warriors for thirty days. During that time they rode 1200 miles, killed thirty-eight people and stole 250 horses and mules, while losing but one warrior...all through a territory infested with eighty three companies of cavalry trying to catch them. The Apaches did not consider Josanie to be a great warrior.

After several months, most of them were back on the reservation with the exception of Geronimo and his band that had been hiding in the Sierra Madres. The army harassed them until Lieutenant Marion Maus was able to get Geronimo to agree to a surrender council. He agreed to meet with General Crook at Canon de los Embudos (which means Canyon of Tricksters). This canyon is about thirty miles from John Slaughter's ranch headquarters and is in Sonora.

Crook told Geronimo the terms: "You must make up your mind whether you will stay on the warpath or will surrender unconditionally. If you stay on the war trail, I will keep after you until I kill every one of you even if it takes fifty years." All the small bands agreed to surrender on the morning of March 27, 1886.

Lieutenant Maus escorted the Apaches to San Bernardino where they would formally surrender to Captain Henry Lawton, who would take them back to the San Carlos Reservation.

An American bootlegger, named Tribolet, met the party near the border and sold whiskey to the Apaches. While they were drinking he convinced them that the moment they crossed the border into the United States they would all be killed. The bootleggers sold a total of fifteen gallons of whiskey which made them thirty dollars. It was not worth the effort but it served a purpose...the purpose of the Tucson Ring, who sold supplies to the military.

Geronimo, Nachez, and thirty-nine other Apaches, well fortified with Tribolet's red-eye disappeared back into the Sierra Madres. General Crook was blamed for their escape, even though he was at Fort Bowie. The incident put him into such a position that he requested that he be relieved of his departmental command.

Crook's successor, General Nelson Miles, received all the credit, fame and promotion for finally obtaining Geronimo's surrender in September, 1886. Ironically Miles had little to do with it. The man, who was responsible for it all, Lieutenant Charles B. Gatewood, received no credit and was transferred to the nether regions by Miles to make sure.

When John Slaughter told Viola about the expected Apache surrender, she and a friend, Emma Ferrington, rushed from Tombstone to the ranch to see it. But, when they arrived, the military would allow them nowhere near the site. Consequently, they did not get to see any part of the surrender.

In 1936 the Marion Williams family of Douglas, Arizona, purchased the ranch. They rebuilt much of that which had been destroyed. Paul and Helen Ramsower eventually became the owners of the San Bernardino ranch.

In 1979, it was purchased by the Nature Conservancy and held in trust until the Fish and Wildlife Service bought it in the spring of 19S2. Their goal is "to preserve, restore and enhance in their natural ecosystem all species of animals and plants that are endangered or threatened with extinction."

The Service wanted the refuge because of the potential as a hatchery for the endangered and threatened species of fish once native to this area: the Yaqui Chub, Yaqui Top Minnow, Yaqui Catfish, and the Mexican Stoneroller. The first two are only about 1 1/2 inches long when they are adults and live only a year or so.

Bird life that flourishes in this region are the Black Bellied Whistling Ducks, Gray and Black Hawks, Caracara, Tropical King Birds, Beardless Flycatchers, and Becards as well as those other species common to southern Arizona.

Also in 1982, 131 acres of the ranch, including the house and outbuildings, were deeded to the Johnson Historical Museum of the Southwest. The San Bernardino ranch has been renovated, named a National Historic Landmark, and is now open to the public. Hundreds of Slaughter family mementos and photographs are on display. A picnic area is located by the lake and the area surrounding the house and lake is a beautiful setting to behold. The view from the front porch into old Mexico in unsurpassed.

The drive from Douglas to this beautiful, historical ranch is a desolate, but a colorful and fascinating trip and the area abounds with deer, javelina, coyote, rabbit, fox and 216 species of birds.

Even today it takes little effort to imagine that you can hear the fearsome cry of the wild Apache and what it was like when John Slaughter built his ranch in the most desolate and dangerous location in the Southwest. You can still feel the terrible loneliness of being miles and miles from anywhere.

Sources:

Cochise County Deeds of Real Estate, Book 123, Page 368

⌒SLAUGHTER, the MAN⌒

John Horton Slaughter was born in Sabine Parrish, Louisiana to Ben and Minerva Slaughter on October 2, 1841. When he was three months old the family moved to Caldwell County, Texas. At the age of fourteen they moved to the vicinity of San Antonio living in Frio and Atascosa counties. John grew up in this savage and merciless land where the settlers were fighting with raiding Comanches, Kiowas, and renegades.

Young John joined the Confederacy on March 29, 1862, in Pleasanton, serving under Captain Lewis Antonio Maverick. He had followed the "Stars and Bars" for the "Lost Cause" but a short time when he was invalided out of service because of tuberculosis. Evidently, he didn't pay heed to his illness as he enlisted in the Texas Rangers and spent full time fighting Comanches and outlaws.

By 1864 he was with Captain J. Brittick in the Third Frontier Division, Texas State Troops quartered in Burnett County. He had served in such companies several times and had gained a reputation as an expert in the use of firearms and that of a fearless warrior.

Ranches were sadly neglected during the War Between the States because of the unavailability of manpower. Cattle ran wild and reproduced at a rapid rate during these war years. By the time the war ended, wild cattle overran the range. It did not take the returning veterans long to realize that these wild cattle were all they had to sell.

John and his two brothers Charley and Billy recorded their ranch in Friotown on September 22, 1871. They called it the San Antonio Ranch Company. By capturing the wild, unbranded cattle they were able to build a herd in a very short while. Their brand was CAV with an earmark.

It was not long until John had his own ranch, located in Frio County. He was not able to long endure partnerships, not even with his brothers. His ranch was stocked with 2,500 to 3,000 head of cattle. Usually, when he started his cattle to market they would number about 500 head. As he passed through other ranches during the drive, his herd would mysteriously increase by strays joining his cattle. When he reached the market and sold his herd they would number 3,000 head. John had a number of road brands and it was not unusual to see cattle with one of these brands in the east to the Brazos River, south to the Gulf of Mexico, north to the Concho, and west as far as Devil's River.

In 1874, Slaughter was given 640 acres of land by the State of Texas. Not long after, they did it again, making a total of 1,280 acres of free land.

Leasel Harris owned a ranch a few miles away, but that was close enough to still be classed as a neighbor. Harris ran about 150,000 head of cattle on his ranch and that number impressed John, but not near as much as did Harris' five foot three inch, blue eyed, blonde and beautiful daughter, Eliza Adeline. The impressive young lady was also a graduate of Edmund's College in San Antonio.

After seeing that lovely young lady, John began to give a lot of thought about being thirty years old and still single. Maybe it was time that he marry and settle down. He began to spend less time with his cattle and more at the Harris ranch paying court to the lovely Eliza. Slaughter seemed to be destined to have problems with mothers-in-law. Eliza's mother was completely horrified when she was informed that John Slaughter wanted to marry her beautiful daughter. She resisted such a union for some time, but John and Eliza were so determined that she reluctantly agreed.

The young couple were married at her parent's home in San Antonio on August 4, 1871. Their first child, Adeline was born there in October, 1872. A boy, Hugh, was born about a year later, but died on John's ranch. Another girl was born to the Slaughters, but she died when she was about one year old. Willie, their last child, was born on December 31, 1877, while John was in Arizona. This child was never strong or healthy.

Being the lone wolf that he was, John had already decided that Texas was overcrowded, and that there was not sufficient land to build the size of ranch that he wanted. While he was traveling through Arizona he had been impressed with the possibilities he had seen there.

Although her last child was just a few months old Eliza went to Friotown to start her preparations for the move to Arizona. John had gone ahead to start a business in Phoenix and to prepare for his family's arrival. Eliza and the two children, Addie who was four, and Willie, the baby, were to make the journey by stagecoach and train.

John had gone by Los Angeles to see a doctor about a cancer that had grown on his hip. The doctor suggested an operation, but John rejected that right away. He insisted on trying a new procedure that he had read about, called the "Kelly Tie Cure". All the doctors advised him against such a move, but John applied the plasters anyway. This procedure proved to be very painful and he began using opium to dull the pain. For nineteen days he suffered the treatments, then the cancerous growth fell out and his hip began the slow process of healing.

What none of the family realized was that a smallpox epidemic was sweeping through west Texas. During the stagecoach rest stops Eliza talked with a lady, who was also traveling west. Eliza did not realize that her newfound friend was infected with the dread disease.

In Phoenix, Eliza became seriously ill in just a few days and no one realized what was wrong with her. Seventeen days after she had left Friotown Eliza died of smallpox. John buried her in Phoenix.

Both children came down with smallpox and John took care of them himself. Phoenix authorities wanted to send them to a "pest house" but John wouldn't hear of it.

No one would come near John or the infected children. Even the doctor left medicine for them at the gate. John applied hot bran poultices on the pustules and tied cloth bags on their hands so they could not scratch them. Eventually, they regained their health.

John Slaughter was not particularly an impressive man in appearance. He was only five feet six inches tall, but he had a thick neck and broad shoulders. His hair, beard, moustache and eyes were all dark. Those who knew him said that he had the most penetrating eyes that they had ever seen.

A man of constant habit, John, never wore Levis or overalls, but always dressed in expensive clothes, and always wore a vest. He had no use for the Mexican spurs with the large rowels, but always wore the small, blunt, military type. Slaughter wore a diamond ring, carried a pearl handled pistol, and rode a gray horse. No notches were on the handles of his six-gun, but legend tells that he killed up to twenty men. No one knew for certain and Slaughter never said.

He had a terrible temper, but most times he kept it under control, though that was often a struggle. A constant smoker, he always had a cigar in his mouth.

Incredible as it may seem, Slaughter firmly believed that he was protected by a guardian angel, and because he was, he could not be killed. It was true that on numerous occasions a mysterious source warned him of impending danger and because he heeded the warning he escaped unharmed. Frequently, he remarked, "No man can kill me. I wasn't born to be killed. I cannot explain it, but I know it. When my time comes, I'll die in bed." The years proved that he was right.

The man did, indeed, bear a charmed life. It was not in the cards for him to die a violent death. The old adage that he who lives by the sword (or gun) shall die by the sword (or gun) somehow did not apply to him.

During the late 1960's many of Slaughter's neighbors, friends, and acquaintances could still be found at the Gadsden

Hotel bar some Saturday mornings. They told many interesting and colorful stories about John Slaughter.

One said, "Yes, I remember Slaughter well. He was a small man and he started almost every statement with 'I say, I say....'"

Another told of:

Slaughter being in a poker game with two strangers. He had been losing steadily until he pulled out his pistol and laid it on the table near his right hand and said, "I say, I say, there does seem to be an awful lot of aces in this deck." It was amazing how his luck changed for the better.

There was another story about the time Slaughter was chasing a bandit. Slaughter was following close behind this outlaw on the trail to Nogales, when he saw a note in the trail, left by the man he was chasing. It read: "I hear that you have made a reputation for yourself as Sheriff of Cochise County. If you want to keep that reputation, get the hell off my trail!"

Slaughter broke for his mount, turned and galloped in the opposite direction. When asked about it he replied, "I say, I say, I know when the hog is fat. If I'd figured he'd rumbled me I'd have gotten off his trail a whole lot sooner!"

One man made an unusual statement, but would not give his name, though he claimed he knew Slaughter personally. From his words and actions he appeared to have a grade school education. His statement was, "Everybody hereabouts knows that John Slaughter's cows were a biological phenomenon".

Such words from him were a surprise, but when asked why he made such a statement he replied, "'Cause all of them cows had eight calves a year!"

John himself, often told the story of how he would notify the customs men at the border that on a certain date he would be bringing fifteen head of cattle from Mexico through Skeleton Canyon into the United States. He knew that there were only two men stationed at the border and that both of them would be there to check his cattle. While they were occupied in Skeleton Canyon he would bring 100 head through someplace else...no check...no duty fees.

That Wicked Little Gringo

A Cochise County cowboy, Leonard Alverson, once revealed just how Slaughter evaded custom regulations. Alverson was working for the Chiricahua Cattle Company (CCC) and he and several other CCC hands had been sent to pick up 2,000 head of cattle that his employers had bought from John Slaughter. When they arrived at the San Bernardino they found John and his hands waiting.

Slaughter had cattle on both sides of the border, but a large number had already been gathered on the United States side. John believed that he would be able to supply all the 2,000 head from this herd. But, as the work progressed, he came up about 300 head short in filling the CCC contract.

He and the CCC hands went across the border, and in about a week's time, they gathered 300 head of the wildest critters to be found anywhere. The cowboys drove them up to the border, but left them in a pasture just south of the line.

That evening two Customs Line Riders came by the ranch. They joined Slaughter and Alverson on the porch. Alverson thought that they were there to inspect and collect the fees for the 300 head that were coming across the border from Mexico.

During the course of the conversation John dropped a hint that he knew for a fact that Concho, (a notorious smuggler), was to cross the border into the States that very night between Silver Creek and Mud Springs. It was said that he was bringing over 100 gallons of mescal with him for sure, and likely a lot of other contraband.

The customs men were all excited and packed up to head for Mud Springs. They told Alverson that they needed him to help them and that he had to go. Slaughter agreed with them and even loaned Alverson his shotgun, saying that customs men had the authority to compel him to help them.

Alverson and the two men patrolled the border between Silver Creek and Mud Springs all night and did not encounter a single person.

When Alverson arrived back at the ranch that morning John smiled and asked him if they had seen any smugglers. But,

Alverson did notice that all of the 300 steers that had been in a pasture in Mexico were now in a pasture in the United States. He knew that it was not his affair, so he kept his mouth shut and started the steers toward the CCC range.

Slaughter once bought a herd of Mexican cattle from the Gabilondo brothers whose ranch was in Mexico. John had always done a great deal of business with this family and there was absolutely no reason why these cattle could not be brought into the United States. However, a customs official, who felt it necessary to demonstrate how important he was refused to let John bring the cattle across the border. Slaughter clamped his mouth shut, said not one word, and drove his cattle out of sight of the border. There, he dispatched a rider and had the Gabilondos come up and take the herd across the border. The same customs inspector, who had refused to let John cross the cattle into the United States, waved the Gabilondos across with a smile.

Once, while riding across his range on the Mexican side John came upon a large corral that held a large number of calves. These calves carried a Mexican brand. What was significant to John was that the mother cows, outside the corral bawling for their babies inside the corral, wore Slaughter's "Z" brand. Whoever had penned them in the corral was trying to wean them before turning them loose.

Before dawn the next morning, John went back to that corral, took down the bars, then drove the sixty calves and their mothers back to the home ranch. Once there, he crossed out the Mexican brand on the calves. then put his own "Z" on the right shoulder.

Marion Williams, who later bought the San Bernardino from the Slaughter family said, "Slaughter wasn't a bad man at all...but he was a very dangerous man...very quick with a pistol. He killed twelve men and they all had it coming. And don't think that most of them weren't damn tough. When Slaughter went after a man he brought him back most of the time dead!"

That Wicked Little Gringo

Once, a breezy stranger, affecting a Southern accent, became too friendly with Slaughter, addressing him as "Tex". Holding up his hand to stop the man's words, John politely said, "My name is Slaughter, sir. If you have reason to address me again, just remember that the name is Mr. Slaughter."

When you quote the men who knew him, some say that John was a good man and some say that he was not such a good man. But, they all agree that he was a man!

One of Slaughter's deputies once commented "Slaughter was a man of few words and he used them damn seldom! He had words for social events, "I'll have the same", and his words for business were "Hit the trail" or "Hands up!"

Jeff Milton, a reputable lawman himself, once said of John Slaughter, "If Slaughter believed that a man needed killing, he thought no more of killing him than putting a hole through a can!"

Slaughter didn't wait for the Apaches to raid him...he raided them! Every time they came near his cattle they paid for it with their blood. Wherever he grazed his cattle he did not allow Apaches. When a roving band appeared in the vicinity, he tracked them down and killed every one of them. As a result of this actions, the fierce Apache changed their war trails into and out of Mexico.

Even the wily Geronimo wanted no trouble with Slaughter and instructed his warriors to ride around the range of that wicked, little gringo and to leave his cattle alone.

While a prisoner at Fort Sill, Oklahoma, Geronimo said that there were only two things he wanted to do before he went to the happy hunting grounds. They were (1) to kill John Slaughter and (2) to die in Arizona.

John Slaughter — age unknown

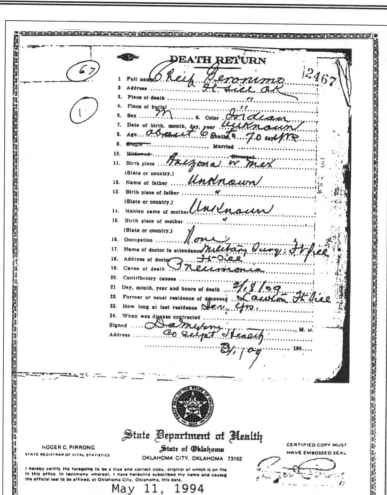

Chief Geronimo' Death Certificate
cause of death — pneuomonia

Enlargement of Certification

KOGER C. PIRRONG
STATE REGISTRAR OF VITAL STATISTICS

State of Oklahoma
OKLAHOMA CITY, OKLAHOMA 73

I hereby certify the foregoing to be a true and correct copy, original of which is on file in this office. In testimony whereof, I have hereunto subscribed my name and caused the official seal to be affixed, at Oklahoma City, Oklahoma, this date.

May 11, 1994

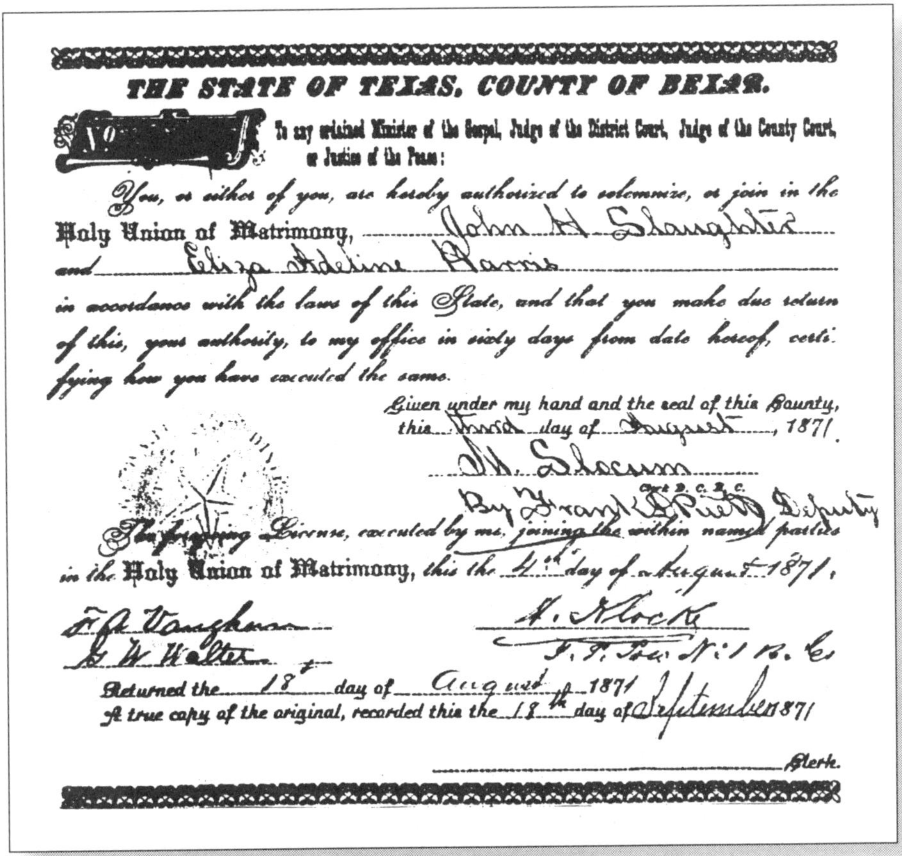

THE STATE OF TEXAS, COUNTY OF BEXAR.

No. To any ordained Minister of the Gospel, Judge of the District Court, Judge of the County Court, or Justice of the Peace:

You, or either of you, are hereby authorized to solemnize, or join in the Holy Union of Matrimony, John H. Slaughter and Eliza Adeline Harris in accordance with the laws of this State, and that you make due return of this, your authority, to my office in sixty days from date hereof, certifying how you have executed the same.

Given under my hand and the seal of this County, this third day of August, 1871.

W. Slocum

Clk D. C. B. C.

By Frank L. Pietz Deputy

The foregoing License, executed by me, joining the within named parties in the Holy Union of Matrimony, this the 4th day of August 1871.

F. A. Vaughan

G. W. Walter

H. Klocke

F. P. Pre. No. 1 B. C.

Returned the 18th day of August 1871

A true copy of the original, recorded this the 18th day of September 1871

Clerk.

Marraige Certificate

John H. Slaughter and Eliza Harris

That Wicked Little Gringo

Jefferson Davis Milton
*Texas Ranger, deputy Sheriff, Stock Association Detective,
Well Fargo Agent, U.S. Customs Border Patrolman, deputy U.S. Marshal,
El Paso Police Chief, and Chinese Agent U.S. Immigration.*

NEW MEXICO & VIOLA

New Mexico first took notice of John Slaughter in the fall of 1876 when he killed Barney Gallagher at South Spring.

While Slaughter was gathering a herd in the vicinity of Devil's River in southwest Texas, "the Man From Bitter Creek" Gallagher had a look at Slaughter's cattle and decided that he would take them.

Gallagher's name and reputation alone would have frightened lesser men, but not one such as John Slaughter. The "Man From Bitter Creek" had reportedly dispatched thirteen men to Boothill and it was obvious that he intended to make Slaughter number fourteen.

Slaughter, a man of few words, observed Gallagher eying his cattle and spoke but three words. "Hit the trail!" With one look into Slaughter's cold dark eyes Gallagher decided that it would be wise to move on and wait for a more opportune time. He rode up into the Fort Sumner country to wait for his intended victim.

John was not fooled by Gallagher, so he took his herd up to the huge Chisum ranch and then waited for word to reach Gallagher that he was there. When the "Man From Bitter Creek" reached Slaughter's herd, he spurred his horse to a full gallop. He was armed with a double barrel shotgun and two 45's. Before he could bring his horse into range of the shotgun, John calmly picked up a rifle and shot the animal from under him.

Gallagher rose from the dust and continued on toward his adversary, a pistol flaming in either hand. However he was still not close enough for accurate pistol shooting and a second shot from Slaughter's rifle broke his arm. A third shot hit him in the stomach and a fourth tore through his lungs.

As he gasped his last few breaths the "Man From Bitter Creek" said, "I needed killing twenty years ago anyway."

When Slaughter sold his herd of cattle in Las Vegas, his count was several head short, apparently lost on the drive. On his return trip to Texas, he cut all the cattle, bearing his brand, from the local herds as was his legal right.

John Chisum, the New Mexico cattle king, was quite perturbed when the brash Texan cut sixty head of cattle from his herd. He objected loudly, claimed that he had bought the cattle, and produced a bill of sale.

Slaughter took one look at the paper and said, "You bought 'em too cheap." Then he rode away, unmolested, with his cattle.

Not long after his wife died John was in Holbrook, Arizona. It was now 1878 and he was waiting to meet a herd of his cattle there. It was here that he first met the Amazon Howell family. He first noticed Cora Viola, the daughter, "riding sidesaddle and helping her father with their stock....her hair flying all about." The Howells were in the process of moving from Nevada to Texas. At the time John did not think he was interested in Cora Viola as a woman, because he thought he would never remarry.

All of the Howells were a close knit clan of hot tempered Southerners. Amazon, the head of the family, was said to be the great grandson of Daniel Boone. Born in St. Charles County, Missouri in 1817, Amazon was raised in St. Louis County, Missouri. His unusual first name was given him by Daniel Boone. His famous great grandfather evidently named him after the Amazon River in Kentucky.

In 1859, Amazon married Mary Ann Tyler, who, though Virginia born, was also raised in St. Louis County, Missouri. Mary Ann was a most beautiful woman, a true belle of Dixie, emotional and high strung. Southern bred and raised, she would sing and dance whenever she heard Dixie.

Cora Viola was born on September 18, 1860. She, too, was brought up faithful to her Southern heritage, as a Dixie belle.

Before the war Amazon had been a successful and prosperous river boat captain and had been called "Cap" by everyone who knew him. He owned a number of riverboats, numerous slaves, and was truly a staunch "Son of the South". All the Howells were dedicated, fervent Confederates, totally loyal to the "Lost Cause", all through the war and even after. Amazon fought with the men in gray. He was captured and put into Yankee prisons nine times, but he escaped each and every time.

Stonewall Jackson was born to the Howells on October 23, 1863. Amazon named him after the Confederate hero, General Thomas "Stonewall" Jackson.

The end of the war brought hard times to the Howells and they lost everything. As they were most eager to improve their status they joined a number of other Missourians on their way to Montana.

Once in Montana the Howells settled in the Gallatin Valley where Amazon did any job that was available. He ran a restaurant, panned gold, and hired out to do anything that paid money.

The move to Montana did very little to improve their lot and none of the family liked it there very much. In 1869 they moved again this time to a farm a few miles from Hamilton, Nevada.

Another baby girl was born to them while in Nevada. Mary Ann, alone except for the children, delivered the baby herself. It was an extremely difficult birth and the baby lived only a few days.

In 1872, a fourth baby, James Alonzo Howell, was born to the family.

That Wicked Little Gringo

Mary Ann was very homesick and became unhappier as time passed. Amazon felt that she would improve if they moved somewhere in the South. She had relatives living in Texas so that is where they decided to go.

Travel was slow and tiresome and the Howells reached New Mexico in the fall of 1878. Three miles west of the Pecos River and about fifty miles south of Roswell, Amazon knew that he had to give his family and his animals a rest. He acquired a few acres of land and began farming.

It was here that they met John Slaughter again. John had decided to move to Arizona and was waiting at the Pecos for his first herd of cattle coming to Arizona from Texas.

Lew Wallace, Governor of New Mexico Territory, ordered the arrest of John Slaughter on March 11, 1879, saying that his reputation in Lincoln County was not acceptable. Lieutenant Bryon Dawson, Ninth Cavalry, arrested John and escorted him to Fort Stanton. Slaughter was dismayed to find that he was accused of stealing twenty-three head of cattle. Actually, he had bought them from Tom Cochran, who had obtained then from a Mrs. Casey. These cattle had been stolen from the John Henry Tunstall estate, but certainly not by John Slaughter.

Governor Wallace had a talk with Slaughter, but was still not very happy with him, as he had Captain Purington put him under arrest and guard on March 25, 1879. Wallace knew full well where the cattle had come from originally and how Slaughter had come by them but Mrs. Casey was unable to provide a valid bill of sale for them. In addition to his other complaints, Wallace was still not satisfied that there had been justification for the killing of Gallagher.

About this time Wallace received a letter from a San Francisco firm, Christy and Wise. They informed him that they had owned a flock of sheep which had been under the care of one Theodore A. Travis. They claimed that Travis had sold the sheep to a man, known to them only as Bob. This Bob had then killed Travis and had stolen both the money and the sheep. They believed that Bob was connected somehow with John Slaughter and that their sheep were now on his ranch near the Pecos River.

Wallace made a list of the men that he thought should be arrested as soon as possible. Slaughter was Number One on this list. How Wallace felt about Slaughter is clearly seen in a report he made to the Secretary of the Interior, Carl Schulz:

"If however, I should be fortunate enough to get all the list, it would be no more than taking the head off the evil. To dig up the roots, it is necessary to crush a number of cattle camps such as Slaughters,, Beckwiths, and thoroughly cleanse the region about the Seven Rivers. These are the places from which the thieves and murderers issue to do their work, and to which, when the work is done, they retire for rest, safety, and to unload their plunder of whatever kind."

It was true that Slaughter did hire the toughest cowboys that he could find. However, he hired a hand for the services that he could do for him and did not care at all about his past record. It was also true that many of the men, who came to Tombstone with Slaughter's cattle herds became outlaws.

Wallace initiated a system whereby all horses and cattle that were not wearing registered brands or were not covered by a certificate of sale would be confiscated and turned over to John Newcomb, County Keeper of Cattle, and whoever had such stock in their possession would be arrested.

John Slaughter was released from custody early in April. He immediately involved himself in more problems of conduct.

On March 19, 1879, William Campbell, accused of murder, and Jessie Evans, also accused of murder, had bribed their guard, Texas Jack, at the Fort Stanton guard house. The three men had then fled the fort. Texas Jack had been captured in a short while. Campbell and Evans had hidden out in Slaughter's cattle camp and when John's herd went on to Arizona they went along with it.

By the time that Slaughter's herd had arrived in New Mexico, John had convinced Amazon Howell that they should throw their herds together and move them to southeast Arizona.

Evidently, there was not enough evidence to bring John Slaughter to trial in Lincoln County. However, he believed that it was in his best interest to get out of New Mexico. So he gathered his cattle and those of Amazon Howell and started them for Arizona.

It seems that Howell also had some problems with Lew Wallace. Amazon had bought his cattle in Nevada and had not obtained the proper bill of sale. Neither had he branded them as Wallace required in New Mexico.

Wallace had a better attitude toward Howell than he did Slaughter and believed that Amazon had legally bought his cattle. But, he believed that if he accepted Howell's story without the required papers, it would set a troublesome precedent; therefore, Wallace had Amazon's cattle placed in Newcomb's custody for a while. Then they were released to Howell but under a bond which required that Amazon present Probate Judge Gonzales a legal and proper bill of sale within three month's time. Slaughter put up the necessary bond for Amazon.

Meanwhile, during the time that John had been with the Howells, he had become quite taken with their daughter, Viola. He had even decided that he might like being married again.

When John informed the Howells that he entertained the thought of marrying their daughter, Amazon was overjoyed. He would relish having John Slaughter as a son-in-law. Mary Ann, however, was totally and absolutely against such a union. She screamed, cried and had hysterics for several hours.

Mary Ann had many reasons why Viola should not marry John. She had not known him long enough. He was too old for her, (John was nineteen years older than Viola). Author's note: (John Slaughter was only four years younger than Many Ann. Ironically, Mary Ann was nineteen years younger than

Amazon). John already had two young children (six years and nineteen months, and she didn't think Viola should be nursemaid and mother to them. She also said that Slaughter was addicted to gambling. Author's note: (John promised Viola that he would quit gambling. It was the only promise to her that he ever broke).

Viola, with her father's blessing, totally ignored her mother's objections and prophecies of disaster and married John Slaughter in Tularosa, New Mexico on April 16, 1879. She was eighteen, John was thirty-seven. Regardless of the age difference and other objections, the marriage lasted for more than forty years. Even Mary Ann developed a healthy respect for Slaughter and came to the point of almost worshiping her tough son-in-law. Believing every word he said, she thought him to be perfect.

WALLACE'S WANTED LIST

1. John Slaughter
2. Andrew Boyle
3. John Selman
4. Selman, John's Brother
5. Gus Gildea
6. Irwin
7. Reese Gobles
8. Rustling Bob
9. Robert Speaks
10. The Pilgrim
11. John Beckwith
12. Jim French
13. Joe Scurlock
14. William Bonney
15. Tom O'Folliard
16. Charles Bowdre
17. Henry Brown
18. John Middleton
19. Fred Waite
20. Jacob Mathews
21. Jesse Evans
22. James Dolan
23. George Davis (aka Tom Jones)
24. Rivers
25. James Jones
26. Williams Jones
27. Marion Turner
28. Caleb Hall (Collins)
29. Haskill Jones
30. Buck Powell
31. James Hyson (Hysaw)
32. Jake Owens
33. Frank Wheeler
34. Joe Hill (Olney)

SOURCES

1. Silver City Herald, October 7, 1876
2. Tombstone by Walter Noble Burns, 1927
3. Cora Viola Slaughter
4. Lew Wallace to Henry Carroll, March 11, 1879. Wallace Collection, IHS
5. Christy and Wise to the governor, New Mexico, March 11, 1879. Wallace Collection IHS
6. Wallace's Wanted List, Wallace Collection, IHS
7. Lew Wallace to Carl Schulz, March 21, 1879. Wallace Collection, IHS
8. Mesilla Independent, May 28, 1879
9. Lew Wallace to I.E. Leonard, April 9, 1879. Wallace Collection, IHS
10. Cora Viola Howell Slaughter
11. Santa Fe New Mexican, July 30, 1877
12. Arizona Daily Star, February 19, 1938
13. Mesilla Independent, April 3, 1879

John Slaughter
Soon after his marriage to Viola

— *from a C.S. Fly Photo*

Viola Howell Slaughter
As a new bride (C.S. Fly Photo)

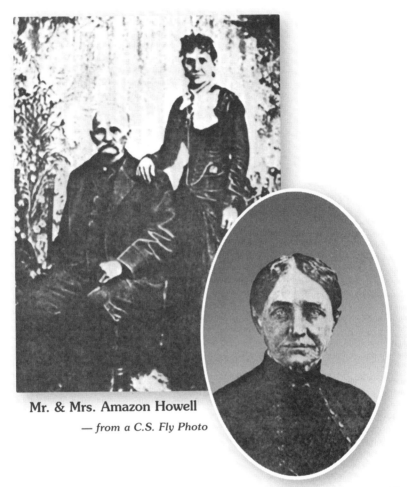

Mr. & Mrs. Amazon Howell
— *from a C.S. Fly Photo*

Mrs. Amazon (Mary Ann) Howell
John Slaughter's Mother-in-law
— *from a C.S. Fly Photo*

Wake Benge, Tal Roland, Jeff Lewis
*Worked as cowboys for John H. Slaughter, July 1879.
All three came to Arizona with Mr. Slaughter's first herd,
Wake Benge and Tal Roland went back for the second herd.*

ON THE SAN PEDRO

The Slaughters and the Howells arrived in the Sulphur Springs Valley in May, 1879. John chose that general area mainly because nearby Tombstone was rapidly becoming a boom town due to Ed Schieffelin's silver discovery in the Tombstone Hills.

Temporarily located, Slaughter sent his cowhands back to Texas to bring his second herd to Arizona. He was kept busy supplying beef to the San Carlos Indian Reservation as per the contract he had made with the Indian Agency.

John seemed to have more trouble with government people than any other. On one occasion at San Carlos, an army officer, who had the responsibility to receive and sign for the cattle delivered, was an obnoxious easterner, who evidently did not know a cow from a bull. To impress his importance to those present, he would randomly single out an animal and say "Reject!" It was obvious to those who knew cattle that there was nothing wrong with that particular animal.

The cowhands and John exchanged knowing looks, but not a word was said. They just drove the rejected cattle back to the herd. However, when they brought up another bunch to be inspected they always included some of the rejects. This time the rejects would be accepted by the brash, young officer. By the time the steers had been selected to meet the contract there would only be five or six rejects left and that was normal.

When John and Viola married, his original plan had been to send his children, Addie and Willie, to Texas to live with his brother. He had told Viola that he did not intend her to be a maid and nurse for his children. They came for a visit in July,

1879, and when it came time for them to go to Texas, Viola told John that she wanted to keep them permanently.

She loved and cared for these children as if they had been her own, and they felt the same way toward her. Whenever he could, John allowed his wife to travel with him on business trips. During these times the children stayed with Mary Ann Howell. The Howell's youngest child, James, was Addie's age.

The Howells had settled at a small spring located between Tombstone and Charleston and had started a small dairy ranch. Amazon would drive about Tombstone and to ranches selling milk to people who had no milk cows. Amazon was a large man with a friendly personality and almost everyone liked him.

The Howell's last child was born while they lived at this location. It was a little girl and it did not live long. They buried this child in the Charleston cemetery near the grave of James C. Howell, Amazon's brother.

After about three months in the Sulphur Springs Valley, the Slaughters moved in August, 1879, to some unclaimed land, located between Charleston and Hereford, a stage stop on the San Pedro River.

Their living quarters were small, constructed by driving tree limbs into the ground, then covering them with mud. The floor and the roof were made of earth, causing all of their crude furniture to always be dirty. Viola had no stove and had to prepare their meals in an open fireplace. Although it was not in the class of a plantation house for an aristocratic Southern belle, Viola managed to make a home for them in those dismal surroundings.

Once they had become settled in their new surroundings, John started a business, a wholesale and retail meat market in Charleston, which was located about ten miles southwest of Tombstone. It was called the Wholesale & Retail Meat Market.

Soon after they had moved to the San Pedro, John took his wife to Tucson to see the Fiesta de San Augustin. Raised as a

Southern lady, Viola was shocked to see the Mexican women drinking, smoking, and gambling in the local saloons. She demanded that John take her back to the hotel at once before someone she knew saw her in such a place and she would be disgraced.

This prudish attitude made her turn down the manager's offer of a box at the Bird Cage Theatre. In later times she had always wished that she had accepted that offer. She never did get to see a play there because of the type of women who began to hang out at the theater.

Viola once rode the stage into Tombstone alone to do some shopping. She wanted to spend the night in town, so she went to the San Jose House to obtain accommodations. The lady who ran the little hotel/boarding house, took one look at this fancily dressed young woman who was unescorted, and told her that there were no rooms available. Viola was mortified that anyone would believe that she was a prostitute. Very carefully she explained who she was.

The woman was very embarrassed. Of course, she knew who the Slaughters were. She explained that when she saw a lone woman get off the stage she decided that she couldn't take her. But there was always a room for Mrs. Slaughter!

After a while they moved into Charleston to be closer to John's business. The town was founded to be a mill town to process the ores from the Tombstone mines. Just across the San Pedro River from Millville, a future merchant of Tombstone, Amos W. Stow, had filed a claim on 160 acres of land on October 28, 1878. The claim he made stated that he desired the land for agriculture and grazing.

On February 1, 1879 Stow had hired a civil engineer, A.J. Mitchell, to survey and lay out a townsite on his 160 acres. The town totaled twenty-six blocks with sixteen lots in each block. The streets were laid out at right angles, those directed north and south being eighty feet wide, and those directed east and west being fifty feet wide. Both Charleston and Millville grew quickly and by May, 1879, about 400 persons lived along the river.

Charleston soon had: four restaurants, four saloons, five stores, two butcher shops, two livery stables, two bakeries, two blacksmith shops, one hotel, one boarding house, one lawyer, one brewery, one barber shop, one doctor, one carpentry shop, one watchmaker, one drug store, one stationery and fruit store, two Chinese laundries, and one brick yard. Charleston never had a church, a bank, or a newspaper.

The saloons never closed, but catered to every whim of the thirsty miners, mill workers, and soldiers. They made available to these customers whiskey, gambling, and painted women.

Considering the kind of town that Charleston was and its location, it is evident that life from day to day was a gamble. Isolated from practically all civilization this rough, young town was in a wild country infested by fierce Apaches. Only a few miles south lay the Mexican border with the country between literally alive with smugglers and bandits. The silver strike in Tombstone had drawn thieves, crooks, and bandits, of all descriptions, as well as gamblers, prostitutes, gunmen, and bleak-eyed killers from all over the world. It was extremely attractive to such people because there was no semblance of law or authority.

It seemed that every killer, gunhawk, rebel, and adventurer in all the west headed directly to Tombstone and Charleston. Of course, there were the hard working mill hands and a sprinkling of settlers, too, but the bad characters far out numbered the good citizens.

There is a Charleston folk story that tells of a man there, a saloonkeeper, who buried his wife one morning, shot and killed a man at noon, and married a new wife that evening.

This, then, was the sort of atmosphere where John Slaughter opened his business and made his home. Still, his business prospered and expanded to where he was supplying meat all along the new Santa Fe (later the Southern Pacific) railroad, which ran between Benson and Nogales.

Curly Bill duly noted Slaughter's presence in his territory, and began to brag in the Charleston saloons that not only would he steal Slaughter's cattle, but that he would sell them right in Charleston. To accomplish this boast, he posted his men in a mesquite thicket that lay in a small valley. When Slaughter's cowboys and cattle came by they would spring their ambush. All they had to do was wait.

The outlaws could see the dust raised by the herd long before they could see the cattle. When the herd came into sight they could see the riders that were keeping the cattle moving. As the herd drew near their place of concealment, the outlaws spurred their horses from the mesquite into a dead run. When all of them were out in the open they were totally amazed to see that Slaughter and ten or twelve of his riders were galloping along the high ground above them shooting at them with rifles! The outlaws realized that they had blundered right into Slaughter's trap. It was perfectly clear to every one of them that anyone who remained in that open valley with those rifles above them would never raid a cattle herd again. They raced across the valley to gain the shelter of the mesquites. By the time they had arrived there all that could be seen of the herd was a dust cloud in the distance.

Curly Bill decided that he would not steal John Slaughter's cattle after all. It was much safer to raid someone who did not have rear guards, scouts, and who did not ride away from their herd to ambush the raiders. In fact, he believed he would feel a great deal safer if he moved his base of operations from Charleston to Galeyville. And he did just that!

There was a tiny settlement between Charleston and Tombstone, most of which was the Brady house. It was called Pick-Em Up because the stagecoach picked up passengers there. Brady, the man who ran a small saloon there, had a large, ugly cancer growing on his lip. John Slaughter used the same treatment on this man's lip cancer that he had used on his hip cancer. This meant the use of plenty of plasters and then using morphine to help Brady with the pain. The procedure worked fine, and the cancer fell off....but so did

Brady's entire lip! Many years passed before nature filled the gaping hole.

Just north of where Slaughter ran his cattle was the ranch of "Old Man" Clanton and his sons. Several head of Slaughter cattle disappeared periodically. John suspected that the Clantons had stolen them, but there was no proof. Then, one day, he caught Ike Clanton on his range.

"If I ever find you or any of your kin on my land again," Slaughter said, "I'll kill you!"

Now that was language that the Clantons understood : they never trespassed again. John's cattle stopped disappearing too.

Viola, who seldom said anything bad about anyone, said in her memoirs, "We knew the Clantons. They were thieves!"

In 1881, John went back to Texas and traded a flock of sheep he owned for cattle. He then brought the herd of cattle to Arizona.

On one occasion John and Viola were driving from Charleston to Calabazas in their buggy. Viola's brother, Stonewall, was with them, riding John's saddle horse. Riding a quarter mile ahead of the buggy he came upon a spring just west of Fort Huachuca. Six saddled horses stood at this watering spot. As Stonewall came closer he recognized Ed Lyell and five of his outlaw friends.

When they heard the sound of the approaching buggy they asked Stonewall who was in it. He informed them that is was Mr. Slaughter and his wife, who were on their way to Sonoita. Lyell and his friends mounted up and rode on up the road.

As the Slaughter buggy passed Igo's ranch three of the men ahead of them went into the ranch house. About a half mile further on there was a steep downgrade. The other three riders sat at this spot, blocking the road. They were trying to force John into a fight over right of way. But, John just turned the buggy out over the steep hillside and went around them.

At the Downing ranch a few miles further on, the Slaughters stopped to spend the night. The next morning they had only traveled a short distance when they came upon three of the men sitting their horses at the top of a small rise.

Viola lost her temper, grabbed the reins from John, and using the whip ran the startled horses straight for the men. She told John to get his gun. Her husband answered calmly, "I say, I say, Viola, I see them. And I always have my gun."

Much to the Slaughters' surprise, when the men saw Viola coming at them in a dead run, they wheeled their horses and fled.

So that John would be ready in the event that they were attacked, Viola drove the buggy the rest of the way. As they neared a section of the road that was flanked by dense trees and growth, John told Viola that in the event of attack he would drop off the buggy and fight from the ground. She was to whip up the horses and get to Calabazas as soon as she could. He reminded her that the men could not kill him. Strangely enough, Lyell and his cohorts disappeared and they saw them no more.

Sometime later, Slaughter heard that Lyell was sick with a bullet wound in the back room of a store in Charleston. John went to see him.

"As soon as you can travel, you leave Cochise County. If I see you again I'll kill you" Lyell's friend, Cap Stilwell was given the same ultimatum. Neither of the men were ever seen in Cochise County again.

Cochise County with numerous canyons, arroyos, and mountains became a rustler's paradise. Cattle could be stolen, branded, then just driven across the Mexican border for a quick sale.

Early on in 1880 a rustler's trail had been defined as running from Old Man Clanton's ranch northeast, close by Tombstone, through South Pass in the Dragoon Mountains, to Soldier's Hole in the Sulphur Springs Valley, to Rustler's Park in the Chiricahuas, and on to Galeyville on their eastern slope. From there it went down to the Animas Valley in New Mexico and to the Mexican border.

Late in 1880, Old Man had turned the ranch on the San Pedro over to his boys and moved over to the Animas Valley in New Mexico, a short distance north of the Mexican Border.

At about the same time the McLaury brothers, Tom and Frank, gave up their water holes on the San Pedro and moved to a ranch near Soldier's Hole in the Sulphur Springs Valley.

With these moves the Clantons now had ranches strategically located in the San Pedro, Sulphur Springs, and Animas Valleys. These places could accept livestock going into or coming out of Mexico, and supply fresh mounts, food, and rest to riders with no questions asked.

Curly Bill had sent a half dozen of his men: Alex Arnett, Jake Gauze, Bud Snow, Jake McKenzie, John McGill, and Milt Hicks into Mexico on a cattle rustling operation. These men had stolen approximately 100 head of cattle in Sonora. It had been a quick strike and they had stampeded the animals through San Luis Pass and into the Animas Valley. Ringo, Tall Bell, Charlie Thomas, Charlie Green, Jim Crane, Billy Lang, Joe Hill, John Greene, and Curly Bill rode over from Roofless 'Dobe Ranch to join the men with the stolen herd.

These cattle were sold to Old Man Clanton. He rested them a bit then headed them to Tombstone, the nearest market, for a quick sale and profit. Six men rode along with him: Dixie Lee Gray, Billy Lang, Bud Snow, Billy Byers, Harry Ernshaw, and Jim Crane; the latter was one of those who had held up the Contention stage, killing Budd Philpot and Pete Roerig in the process on March 15, 1881. Warrants were out for his arrest and Wyatt Earp wanted desperately to capture him.

The planned route of travel was from Old Man Clanton's ranch through Guadalupe Canyon into the San Bernardino Valley, through the Sulphur Springs Valley around the Dragoon Mountains into Tombstone. The first night they bedded down the herd in Guadalupe Canyon about one mile south of the

International Border, near the area where Arizona, New Mexico, Sonora, and Chihuahua meet.

The next morning, August 13, 1881, as the men were getting breakfast, they were fired upon by ambushers, killing Gray, Crane, Clanton, Snow, and Lang. Only Byers and Ernshaw escaped with their lives. Some say they were killed by Mexican soldiers, others say that perhaps the Earps were involved.

John Slaughter was on very friendly terms with Emilio Kosterlitzky, who was chief of the Rurales, so most likely he knew exactly what happened. Slaughter commented very little about anything, but he was no fool, he knew that except for Virgil, all the Earps, Doc Holliday, and their gunmen friends were missing from Tombstone when Clanton and his men were gunned down. Possibly he was elated to watch them kill each other. It is certain that his sharp eyes watched the Earp posse return to town and observed that Holliday and Warren Earp were no longer with them.

Slaughter's smile must have become much wider on October 26, 1881, when the Cowboys and the Earp faction clashed again. He must have been quite amused to watch the Cowboys set up a plan to kill Doc Holliday and have it backfire on them. Then, when they tried to back away from it, Doc pushed them into a gunfight where they lost three men, Billy Clanton and Tom and Frank McLaury. That made a total of eight men that the Cowboys had lost in a little over two months. Well, Slaughter wouldn't miss any of those rustlers, neither would his cows.

In 1883 John decided that he was going to move to Oregon and establish a cattle ranch on the Snake River. He sold all of his cattle to William Lang, a rancher in the Animas Valley. John, Viola, and the two children took the train from Arizona to Salt Lake City, then traveled from Ogden to Boise City, Idaho by stagecoach. This portion of the trip took five days and four nights. At one stage stop, the station agent informed John that it was a very bad area and that there were always a number of disreputable characters in and out. He said that if John had money he should give it to the stage driver for safe keeping. Slaughter replied that he had no money, but that if he had, he was perfectly capable of protecting it himself. Actually, he had a great deal of money in a belt around his waist, in fact, all of the money they had in the world. He knew badmen well enough to know that if any thieves did show up, he would be their target; therefore, he gave the money belt to Viola and she wore it for the remainder of the trip.

They discovered later that the station agent was working with a band of thieves. He would find out which passengers were carrying money, then inform his cohorts in crime.

The original plan had been for two of the Slaughter's employees to meet them with a wagon and horses in Boise. John and his family arrived first, but before the ranch hands got there John had a severe hemorrhage. Following a lengthy discussion John and Viola decided that with the health problems that John was experiencing they had better return to Arizona.

One of the two cowhands was sent back to Arizona by stagecoach. The other, Tad Rowland, drove the Slaughters back to Silver City, New Mexico. Tad Rowland, who had come from Texas with John's first herd, was one of Slaughter's most loyal employees. Once, John had sent Rowland to collect money that was owed him. Rowland collected $500 for Slaughter, but, on the way home, stopped off for a rest in Charleston. Somehow, all of John's money disappeared. It was several days before Rowland returned to the ranch and he had no idea as to what had happened to him. Likely, he was drugged then robbed. He explained what had happened the best he could to John, then said he would work without wages until it was paid back...and he did that although his pay was only thirty-five dollars a month.

This unfortunate young man had rheumatism that sometimes crippled him. Slaughter frequently sent him to the hot springs to take the baths. They helped, but only temporarily.

His affliction grew worse and he died in 1888 at the age of thirty-four years. John Slaughter was with him in his last hours.

John stopped off in Silver City and stayed for a while. He managed to obtain a contract to supply beef to the railroad that was being built across New Mexico and Arizona.

Leaving John in Silver City, Viola and the children continued on to her parent's milk ranch. When John returned to Arizona the family moved to Tombstone, into a house which was located at the southeast corner of Fremont and First streets. John continued buying and selling cattle and soon opened a meat market in Tombstone.

Along with other ranchers in southeast Arizona, Slaughter lost a lot of cattle to rustlers. Some he lost to the Apaches, but that slowed somewhat when the Chiricahuas were exiled to Florida. Along with the Apaches were two other classes of rustlers. There were the full time thieves whom everyone knew, and the thieves who professed to be honest ranchers.

Laws were not rigidly enforced and crime flourished throughout the county. Thieves and murderers used Tombstone's Whiskey Row as their headquarters and playground. Sick and tired of fear and violence, local citizens reached out to John Slaughter in desperate need. They believed that he was the only one with the nerve, determination, and ability to clean up southeastern Arizona.

John was busy with his own enterprises and therefore reluctant to take on such a difficult task. However, he agreed to run for the position of Sheriff of Cochise County, and was elected on the Democratic ticket in 1886. Slaughter was to serve two terms as Cochise County Sheriff and his time of service has gone down in Arizona history as outstanding.

Gravestone *of James C. Howell, a relative of the wife of Sheriff John Slaughter, is almost forgotten in Charlestson cemetery.*

James Potter
*Came to Tombstone in 1881 with the
third herd of cattle John Slaughter brought from Texas*

— from a C.S. Fly Photo

James Howell, Stonewall Howell & Jesse Fisher

— from a C.S. Fly Photo

Grave *of Charles Howell in the Charleston Cemetery. He was Viola's youngest brother.*

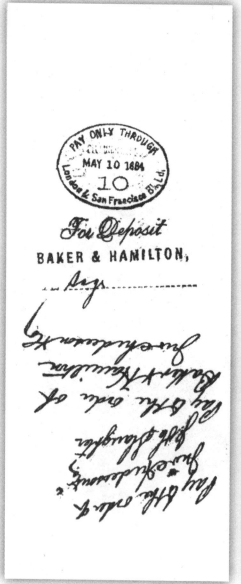

> The Bank of California
> San Francisco, June 4th 1886.
>
> Cashier
> Cochise County Bank Tombstone A.T.
> Dear Sir, We acknowledge receipt of your favors of 28th, 29th, 30th & 31st ulto. contents of which have our due attention.
>
> We credit you for remittance.
> As per your letters
> $ 502.55
>   4267.50
>   1138.30
>   434.50
> $ 6,332.65
>
> We charge your a/c
> Credited & advised Bank of Tucson $ 1000 —
> your telegram received
> We have forwarded to Mr. John H. Slaughter Nogales, A.T. $ 3400 Mexican, and charge your a/c as per enclosed a/c $ 2767.10
> N.T.& Co's receipt herewith.
>
> Yours truly
> For Cashier
> J. Dunn

SHERIFF of COCHISE 1887-1890

Cochise County ranchers always wanted to buy cheap cattle; therefore, they were not too picky as to who was selling them or where they came from. Sometimes, when the rustlers needed a quick sale, ranchers might buy an entire herd for five dollars a head, no questions asked. Politics anywhere are always strange, but in Tombstone politics were unbelievable. Author's note: (Our state legislature even today refers to us as "the country of Tombstone".) John Slaughter was not involved in the politics of Tombstone for many years. He did not take sides in the Cowboy Earp feud. In fact, he and both sides studiously avoided each other. Slaughter made a most unusual sheriff. He did little of what was expected. He did not increase the number of deputies nor did he lead posses on a chase, usually he would take two deputies along at most.

His courage and determination made him a man of iron a loner, silent, dangerous, and deadly. Frequently, he would advise his deputies, "I say, I say, shoot first and yell....throw up your hands afterwards!"

He was a man of few words, taciturn, but not surly, direct, blunt and to the point under any circumstances. He was never known to argue or waste time talking. When he gave a command that was always his final word, there was no appeal. The accused could only accept his challenge or obey his command. Some of his adversaries retreated, some did not.

Sheriff Slaughter was not hesitant to say that he had little faith in courts and juries. Many times, in dealing with the criminal element, he did not remember that he was only an officer of the law. At times, he became the law itself, frequently acting in the capacity of judge, jury and executioner.

That Wicked Little Gringo

The theft of a horse was not always a capital offense in the eyes of the law, but Slaughter had a different attitude. When it was reported to him that a horse had been stolen, he would ride out on his gray and in a few days or a week, he would return leading the stolen animal. Never once did he fail to bring back the horse, but no one ever saw him bring back the thief. Evidently, that particular undesirable was numbered among the permanently absent. John never said what had happened to them and no one asked.

No grand jury ever asked John about those that were missing, nor did any citizen. No one asked John Slaughter questions. It did no good to ask, and besides that, it was downright dangerous. During that period of time justice was not too formal. All law abiding people were just glad that the undesirables were gone, never to return.

Slaughter was always a man of mystery. His personality and actions were so unpredictable that no one could understand them. Some things he did on a regular basis, such as: carry his gold in a money belt, always sat at the end of a table, and was always up and dressed before sunrise. Then he did other unusual things such as: change horses for no reason, change his plans at the last moment, change his route of travel, and speed up or slow down his travel time.

It is true that all the major gunmen of Cochise County were long gone when Slaughter agreed to get rid of the' bobtail leftovers. Tombstone's boom was over and the high rollers, card sharks, and killers had long gone on to Deadwood or other boom towns, or had been killed or chased out by the Earps and Holliday.

Still the county had enough of the criminal persuasion to keep an honest sheriff busy full time. True, the bank holdup artists and the train robbers were of small caliber, but sometimes, they were quite deadly. Travelers were being robbed and sometimes murdered. Mexican banditos were invading Arizona to escape the Rurales. Rustlers were stealing cattle and horses from both countries. Slaughter was the sheriff, who would give

Tombstone's last outlaws a deadline to hit the trail. He would bury the ones who did not heed his ultimatum.

When he took office John appointed some good men to assist him. Enoch A. Shattuck was named under sheriff. G.W. Farrington became a deputy and jailer in Tombstone. As he felt the need John appointed more deputies: James Scow, Edward R. Monk, D. Johnson, Ed Barker, and W J. Showers.

Slaughter appointed a number of his in-laws to support his office. Most likely he did so because he knew them well and recognized their ability to do the job he wanted. Tommy Howell, Stonewall Howell, and Jesse Fisher became part of the sheriff's office.

One deputy that Slaughter appointed that he likely regretted was Burt Alvord. Any mention of Alvord in later years would bring out John's temper. He would soundly curse that renegade ex-lawman.

Outlaw that he became, it still has to be said that for as long as he was John's deputy, Alvord was loyal to Slaughter and the public that he served.

Burt had arrived in Tombstone in the early 1880's with a seriously ill mother, a father who liked hanging out in saloons much better than working, and a teenage sister who desperately tried to hold the family together. Mrs. Alvord died about two years after coming to Tombstone. With little or no guidance, Burt spent most of his time doing odd jobs for John Montgomery at the O.K. Corral or in the local billiard parlors where he was able to make a little spending money.

When John deputized Burt, Alvord was about twenty years old. He was dirty, vulgar, ignorant, and played around with the Mexican girls when he had the money to spend on them. But Burt was tough as iron, not fussy about eating or sleeping regularly, was a fine fighter, and had a sense of humor. All the latter were the qualities that impressed Slaughter. Also in his favor, Burt was at home in the desert and mountains. He was able to find trails that were nonexistent and stick to them.

"By God, I say, I say, Burt's there! I say he's there!", Slaughter said in praise of Burt's ability in rough country.

When John took office in 1887, Alvord was a local character, who avoided any sort of hard labor, but always seemed to have money. He was on friendly terms with everyone from known outlaws to Billy Hildreth, who was one of Slaughter's ranch hands. The sheriff probably reasoned, and rightly so, that Burt would be a vast source of information about his lawless friends.

It still appears that John did not totally trust Alvord. Billy Breckenridge once said, "John told Burt to never walk behind him, that he would kill him if he did. And maybe he would have."

Viola would have had many sleepless nights had she known then that Burt would later turn outlaw. Fortunately, she saw him as a kind and thoughtful fellow, who took good care of her husband. A man, who always carried a coat and muffler in the event the weather might turn cold and his boss would need them if he had an asthma attack.

A bit of evidence here and a word of information there gained by Slaughter's deputy, Burt Alvord, finally pointed the finger of suspicion to Juan Soto as the leader of the rustlers and thieves operating around Tombstone and Charleston. One day, word came to the sheriff's office that two cattle buyers had been robbed and murdered near the Mexican border.

Slaughter had hard evidence that Soto had been in that area on the night that two men had been murdered. Soto was arrested and it appeared to be a good solid case. John told the court that he had spent several nights following Soto and that he was an eye witness to Soto's presence in the murder area where the cattle buyers had been killed. He also presented evidence that Soto had been a member of a bandit gang in California; however, a disinterested jury was swayed by Soto's lawyer and rendered a verdict of not guilty. Juan Soto, a big smile of his face, left the courtroom a free man.

Slaughter had had enough of judges and juries finding verdicts of not guilty when he knew that the defendants were guilty. So, he formed a one man law and order committee and this committee rode down to Contention. He was absolutely positive that Soto was guilty of the majority of the crimes that had been committed in the area.

He rode right up to Soto's front porch. Soto came out, a smirk on his face. Pointing a forefinger at him, Slaughter said, "If I ever see you in this county after today, I'll kill you!"

Soto talked and blustered in the local saloons about how Slaughter could not run him out of the county. But, when the deadline arrived, Soto was not to be found.

Van Wyck Coster was another bandit kingpin in the Willcox area of the Sulphur Springs Valley. This particular man wielded so much political power and had so much money that everyone believed him to be completely immune to legal procedures.

John did not waste time or money in the arrest and trial on this character. Instead, he rode right up to Coster's house and said, "I have known what you are doing for quite some time." He listed the crimes that Coster had committed to justify what he was saying, then he delivered the same ultimatum that he had given to Soto, "Get out of this county or I'll kill you!" Coster, much to the surprise of everyone took the advice and disappeared forever.

Sheriff Slaughter, accompanied by Constable Fred Dodge and Charlie Smith went to Contention and at the slaughtering establishment of L.Larrieu, arrested him, his son John, and three of his employees, John Foster, John Galin, and Rafael Varela, (the latter, was better known as Chappo). They were all arrested on a charge of alleged cattle stealing made by John Vaughn of the Vail Cattle Company.

Vaughn had been informed by an unnamed party that he had seen a cowhide, bearing the Vail brand at Larrieu's place of business. Since he knew that his company had not sold

Larrieu any cattle, Vaughn had gone to the pen and found the cowhide bearing the Vail brand. Then he had gone to Tombstone and lodged his complaint.

Although the slaughterhouse was strongly suspected of slaughtering rustled Vail Cattle Company beef, there was not sufficient evidence for a conviction.

In April, 1887, George Cleveland stole a horse from the Grand Central Mine. Constable Bill Showers captured him in the San Pedro Valley.

Cleveland claimed that he had bought the horse from a Mexican who was on his way to Sonora. Slaughter and Judge Richard Sloan had heard that alibi many times. It had been used so many times that locals, not wishing to tell all the truth, would say in jest, "I bought it from Manuel."

The judge gave him quick justice and Cleveland was sentenced to a year in Yuma.

By the time that he had been sheriff for three months, Slaughter had nineteen prisoners in the county jail. Local citizens had already begun to refer to it as the Hotel de Slaughter.

In May 1887, Sheriff Slaughter brought in Juan Lopez, who was charged with murder. Two years before, an old man named Grout, who had a a milk ranch near the Golden Rule Mine in the Dragoons, was found dead in his cabin from gunshot wounds. It was evident that he had been dead for two or three days.

The old man was known to have some cash money. At about the same time that he was found dead, his money, horse, saddle, and his employee, Juan Lopez, were also found to be missing. It appeared that Lopez was the guilty party.

After Slaughter had arrested him, Lopez confessed before witnesses that he had killed Grout because the old man owed him money for work that he had done, but had refused to pay him.

Following the killing, Lopez took the murdered man's horse and rode into Sonora. It was not long until he was in trouble there and was sentenced to a jail term. The authorities in Cochise County were notified of Lopez's whereabouts, but for some strange reason took no action. (This occurred some time before John Slaughter became sheriff.)

When Lopez had served his time and was released he went into the horse stealing business. Once he made a big raid and acquired twenty-two head of fine animals. He headed north to sell them in Arizona, but encountered the Rurales. They chased him, but he managed to elude them although they forced him to abandon his herd of stolen horses. He had one other bit of bad luck. The Rurales chased him right across the border into Graham County, Arizona. Lopez was arrested almost immediately on a minor offense and drew a sentence of thirty days. John Slaughter heard about where he was. He went to Solomonville and brought the prisoner back to Tombstone.

Locked in the local jail, Lopez told a lady visitor that he had killed Grout. As he had attended the local public schools, a number of his schoolmates came to see him. To one of them he said that he expected to be sentenced to about four years in the Territorial Prison at Yuma, but he did not really care so long as he did not receive a life term.

Lopez changed his plea from "not guilty" to "guilty of murder in the second degree". He also claimed that Grout had shot at him twice before he killed him.

His plea change saved him from the rope, but on May 28, 1887, he was sentenced to fifteen years in the Yuma Penitentiary.

During August of 1887, a man named Carmen Mendibles stabbed Thomas Salcido through the heart during an argument in a house of ill fame. Though the deed was done in Fairbank, the culprit fled to Sonora where the minions of Cochise County law could not arrest him.

Sheriff Slaughter knew where he was and just bided his time until his man crossed the border again. Lo and behold, when Mendibles did cross, it was near the San Bernardino ranch and the sheriff was waiting for him.

The prisoner in custody was described as about thirty years old, and a good looking Mexican. Reports say that he was one tough customer that put up a desperate fight and had to be subdued, chained, and handcuffed. As soon as he was locked behind bars, he became docile and refused to say anything.

It seems that Mendibles' entire family were wild and strange people. The father was a native of Sonora. His name was Carmen and he had six sons, all of which he had named Carmen because he, the father, worshiped Nuestra Sonora del Carmen. Carmen, son 1, had been shot: Carmen, son 2 had been hanged: Carmen, son 3, was in John Slaughter's jail waiting transportation to Yuma: and Carmen, the father, had killed his wife with an axe. The fate of the last three sons is not known.

On November 16, 1887, Sheriff Slaughter and Deputy Stonewall Howell transported four prisoners, Jerry Barton, Carmen Mendibles, Jesus Flores, and Estrado to prison. They were convicted of various offenses at the last term of court. They were sentenced to Yuma for terms ranging from two years to a life sentence. Deputy Tad Rowland accompanied them to the rail head at Benson.

Augustin Chacon was probably the only outlaw that was able to upset John Slaughter. Chacon was described as powerfully built with long arms and huge hands. At times he boasted a bushy beard and during these times he was known as Peludo, (the hairy one).

Chacon and Slaughter hated one another for no obvious reason, but hated enough to strive mightily to kill each other. Chacon was bold enough to challenge Slaughter by coming to Tombstone one night.

The sheriff knew where Chacon was holed up, so he took his shotgun and Deputy Alvord along. They crept slowly and quietly up the dry wash located back of the courthouse. The two lawmen came to a tent lit by a single candle. Slaughter told Alvord to go to the front of the tent, take cover, and then call out to Chacon that he was under arrest. Meanwhile, the sheriff would be at the back of the tent in the event that Chacon tried to escape. Alvord did as he had been ordered, and Chacon did as expected and bolted through the back of the tent. The deputy heard Slaughter's shotgun blast through the darkness. When he reached the rear of the tent he fully expected to see Chacon laid out, bloody and dead. Instead, he saw his boss, cursing and stamping about.

Angrily, Slaughter explained that when Chacon came rushing out, he had tripped over a tent wire and tumbled headlong into the dry wash, causing Slaughter's shotgun blast to miss him completely. Chacon had been wise enough to leave a horse tied in the wash. It had been simple to ride off down the wash, completely out of the sheriffs sight the entire way.

Chacon and Slaughter never saw each other again, but they heard a great deal about one another over the the next few years. In 1895 Chacon robbed a store near Morenci which was owned by a Mrs. McCormick. The manager, Paul Becker, had refused to open the safe and Chacon killed him in cold blood. A posse ran Chacon and his men to ground and had them surrounded. Pablo Salcido, an old friend of Chacon's came out in the open in an attempt to get him to surrender. Chacon murdered Salcido for his trouble. During the gun battle that ensued, Chacon was wounded twice.

Unable to ride, he was captured and lodged in the Solomonville jail. A quick trial found him guilty of murdering Becker and he was sentenced to hang. Chacon boasted that he had killed fifteen Americans and thirty seven Mexicans.

Just ten days before he was to be hanged, on June 9, 1897 he escaped jail with the help of a Mexican lady friend who smuggled him a hacksaw blade. Chacon fled to Sonora and managed to evade arrest for five years.

Burton Mossman, Captain of the Arizona Rangers, enlisted the aid of Burt Alvord to help him capture Chacon. Alvord by now was an outlaw and escaped prisoner. Mossman pretended to be an outlaw and invaded Chacon's hideout with Alvord. When an opportunity presented itself, he arrested Chacon and rode out of Mexico with the killer in handcuffs.

By sheer chance, Mossman, with Chacon in tow, met the Graham County sheriff at the Benson train station. The sheriff was very happy to take custody of the surly prisoner.

Chacon was hanged at Solomonville on November 22, 1902. His last words were, "I consider this to be the greatest day of my life." John Slaughter agreed wholeheartedly.

Although Mossman had brought Chacon out of Sonora alive he had, in truth, kidnapped a Mexican citizen. So he slipped out of Bisbee and went north to Holbrook. There he caught a train to New York to visit his old friend, Colonel Bill Greene. If the Mexican government wanted to arrest him they would have to locate him first. Before he left, he gave his favorite horse to John Slaughter.

Slaughter received information that several train robbers, who had held up a train at Papago early in August, 1887, were holed up at Hughes' Ranch near Stein's Pass. The sheriff and Constable Fred Dodge rode horses to Dragoon Summit where they boarded a special car provided them by the railroad. At Willcox they picked up Deputy Sheriff Robertson, then continued on to Stein's Pass.

When the lawmen arrived at Hughes' Ranch they were able to surprise the outlaws. Hughes escaped, but the other four were captured. One managed to get into the clear temporarily, but John Slaughter's horse was able to run him down. When the sheriff zinged two shots close by his ear, the man gave up.

When Slaughter and his men boarded the train at Stein's Pass, they had in custody, J.T. Blunt, Dick Johnson, Joseph Brooks, and Larry Sheehan. Residents of Lordsburg, New Mexico who knew the four men arrested, said that they might steal a horse or a calf, but didn't think that they were capable of anything beyond such petty thievery.

Jack Martin had a wife that he had brought from Texas some years back. He owned mining interests in Nacozari, plus he also owned a butchering business. All these business interests kept him away from home a great deal, and his wife, Tommy, had the feeling of being neglected.

Apparently tired of being ignored by her husband and having no desire in being a homebody, Tommy took up with Charles Williams. Williams, described as a small man, about twenty-eight years of age, had been employed by Jack Martin as a utility man about the ranch for the past few months.

Tommy Martin, the woman in this case, was well known to just about everyone in the vicinity. She was always dressed in boys clothes and usually had a chew of tobacco in her mouth. Her age was about thirty years and she weighed around ninety pounds. She was known to be an expert with horses and firearms.

Her husband, Jack, had been a participant in the Lincoln County War on the same side as Billy the Kid. He was known to be generous to a fault and good natured, except when aroused. Then, he became a very desperate and dangerous man.

Tommy reasoned, probably correctly, that her husband would not be overjoyed at her liaison with the hired help, so she talked Williams into running away with her. To make the venture more enticing she took $3,000 in gold coins, (which made up the payroll for Jack's mines), a gold watch and chain, his two best horses, and his dog.

When Jack discovered that the guilty couple had fled, taking his money and his animals, he went in pursuit of them. Meanwhile, the couple had become lost and did not reach Charleston until sometime the next day.

Later that day Williams went into Fairbank to buy some shoes for Tommy. While there he learned that Martin had arrived and was looking for him and the woman.

Williams quickly left Fairbank, but Martin heard about it and took his trail. He followed his employee into a canyon, located about four miles from John Hill's ranch on the San Pedro River. Jack Martin was killed in this canyon.

Sheriff Slaughter, Captain Kelton, and four men set out in pursuit of the killers. The end of the trail was expected to be a bloody affair, as both the man and woman were heavily armed and had vowed not to be taken alive. Predictions had been made that Sheriff Slaughter and his posse would either capture them or kill them!

Dr. Dunn held an inquest on the body of Jack Martin. Items found in his pockets were a plug of tobacco, matches, one pistol cartridge, and a note written in pencil, "Passed Fairbank this evening of the 25th pursuing outlaws, a man, a woman, and a dog. Any news later telegraph at once. A.J. Martin".

Dr. Dunn stated that the corpse had three bullet wounds, one though the left elbow, another entered the right hip, carrying with it a rivet from Martins overalls. The third bullet struck him in the left side just below the arm pit, passing through the heart and lungs. The latter shot caused instantaneous death in Dr. Dunn's opinion.

The general impression the inquest panel had was that Martin had been shot by both the man and the woman. For whatever reason, they had also shot and killed Martin's dog.

It was ruled by the inquest that Jack Martin had met his death by gunshot wound inflicted by Charles Williams and Tommy Martin.

The trail led John Slaughter through a wild, rough section of high desert country, which included the Galiuro, Rincon, and Pinal mountains. They quit only when men and horses wore out. Slaughter said that the two fugitives had an abundance of money and that the Mexicans were protecting them. He predicted that they would come out of the mountains and surrender soon.

At this time a strange item appeared in an issue of the Tombstone Prospector:

"We would suggest to Sheriff Slaughter that he be a little more careful in the selection of his deputies. 'He has made the best Sheriff the County ever had' is heard on every hand, and is, in the opinion of this paper, a model sheriff, but in the appointment of his deputies outside of the courthouse he has placed confidence in men, who should, themselves, have been placed in an insane asylum long ago."

An Army patrol in May, 1888, found a dead body just across the canyon from Pyeat's Cave, which is located near the west gate of Fort Huachuca. The body had been hidden under a cut bank and covered with blankets, rags, and a thin layer of dirt. An April 20, 1888 copy of the Police Gazette, said that a white hat, saddlebags of food, a bridle, and a pack saddle were with the body.

The Army captain made a long and flowery report for the county coroner, stating that the remains were filled with maggots and that the corpse was assumed to be Mexican. The report also stated that the mystery man had died of natural causes. Also included was a statement that a new, expensive Dutch oven was found not far from the body. The soldiers in the patrol examined the remains, then buried them.

Sheriff Slaughter read the Army report and knowing the Mexican people as he did, could not accept it. He knew that when Mexicans traveled about looking for work, their camp outfit consisted of little more than a serape and a small bag of corn meal, which whey would bake on a flat rock by the fire.

John swore in W.H. Constable, J.M. Empey, Frank and Tom Frary, and J.S. Taylor to act as a coroner's jury and these men went out to view the remains and make an inquest.

In spite of the maggots they carefully examined the body and discovered that the cause of death was a skull fracture on the right side of the head. The jury was not able to identify the murdered man, nor could they name his killer. They did know

That Wicked Little Gringo

that he was not killed by Mexicans or Apaches. Either of these would have taken all of the fine camp equipment and food even the dead man's clothes.

The army patrol had buried the corpse only a foot deep. Slaughter and his jury dug a proper grave, reburied the victim and covered the site with rocks to keep the animals out. They put up a marker which read: "Name Unknown, Died May 1888". The marker and grave have long since disappeared. This crime was never solved.

On May 11, 1888, six outlaws held up a northern Mexico and Arizona train at the Agua Zarca station. During the robbery they shot and killed the engineer, fireman, conductor, and the express messenger.

The gang involved was the Jack Taylor gang. A short time after the holdup, Taylor, the leader of the gang, and a German, called Fritz, were arrested in Nogales while buying a three dollar hat. They were quickly tried and sentenced to one of Mexico's unpleasant penitentiaries.

On December 16, 1889, the Prospector carried an article on the Mexican execution of Jack Taylor. The description of the execution read: "Preparations were quickly made and two minutes later Taylor, supported by two policemen, stepped into the dark graveyard. His legs carried chains, the remarks that Taylor made were uncomplimentary to gringos. It must be said that Taylor died bravely. At 4:45 the executioners fired four shots and a second later, a mercy shot was sent into the brain. All four shots by the firing squad were in the breast.

Taylor requested that his boots be removed and that he not be blindfolded. His requests were granted. After the doctor pronounced life extinct, he was buried immediately. There was no minister or priest present."

That left four of the Taylor gang running loose. Word was about that they had been seen in the Whetstone Mountains. These outlaws were Nieves Deron, Geronimo Miranda, Manuel Robles, and Frederico Acuna. Mean, tough characters, they were all wanted by the Mexican Rurales and a number of Arizona sheriffs.

Some of these men had kinfolk around Tombstone, so they tried to hide out right in Slaughter's backyard. Of course, Slaughter soon heard that all four of them were hiding in the home of a woman named Flora Cardenas. She was feeding and bedding them when Slaughter and his men slipped in from the mountains. Deputies staked out the adobe house of Mrs. Cardenas for several days, but someone had warned the outlaws. When the sheriff questioned the woman she indignantly denied everything. New reports came in that the killers were holed up at Clifton, then at Willcox. Deputies could find no trace of them at either place. Their trail was ice cold.

Then the sheriff learned that Manuel Robles had a brother named Guadalupe, who sold firewood in the little town of Contention on the San Pedro River. Guadalupe's source of wood supply was a wood camp that he ran in a canyon of the Whetstones called French Joe Canyon. He bought his supplies at a small general store in Contention. An informant reported to the sheriff that Guadalupe, who lived alone, had begun buying more groceries than any one man could eat within a reasonable time.

During a rosy Arizona sunrise, Slaughter and deputies Burt Alvord and Cesario Lucero surrounded the wood camp. They found three of the outlaws still rolled in their blankets. The sheriff recognized them as Nieves Deron, Manuel Robles, and Guadalupe Robles, who was guilty of nothing except harboring the fugitives, one of whom happened to be his brother.

"Roll out and throw up your hands!" the sheriff shouted.

The bandits rolled out all right, but with guns blasting in their hands. Slaughter's first shot killed Guadalupe Robles, the wood cutter. Manuel Robles and Nieves Deron raced for the cover of a pile of boulders, the sheriff's bullets slicing the air around them.

When they reached the rocks, Deron turned and fired three times. One of his bullets grazed Slaughter's ear....blood ran down his cheek. Slaughter's next shot knocked the man down, mortally wounded.

Manuel Robles, terrified now by the shooting of his brother and companion, raced down a wash. Burt Alvord shot at him several times, but missed him by a wide margin.

Slaughter called out to Alvord, "I say, I say, Burt, you're shooting too high! Pull down! I see that you are raising dust beyond him every time!"

The sheriff's next shot knocked Robles down. Cursing and bleeding Robles leaped to his feet. A shot by the sheriff knocked him down again. Incredibly, the Mexican jumped up again and disappeared into the mesquite as Slaughter's next shot missed him completely. Lucero tracked the wounded Robles for some distance by the blood he was losing, but finally lost the trail.

Deron, badly wounded, was taken from Fairbank to Nogales, where he was to be turned over to the Mexican authorities. He died while en route to Nogales, just before the train reached Crittenden. To the last he refused to give the names or any of the particulars concerning his companions in the train robbery. He did admit that he was one of the party, and that he had shot the fireman.

Three of Jack Taylor's gang were still at large, Geronimo Miranda, who for some reason had managed to be absent during the gun battle in the Whetstones. Frederico Acuna, who had also been absent, and the seriously wounded Manuel Robles.

One newspaper article in 1888 which showed that Sheriff Slaughter did try to solve all the crimes in his county read:

"Sheriff Slaughter recovered two burros yesterday which had been stolen some time ago from Don Jose Maria Elias. They were found in the Dragoon Mountains and were being used for packing wood."

Another such article shows that he did not forget crimes that had been committed before his term of office:

"Burt Alvord returned from the Gila River country Wednesday night, bringing back with him six head of horses that were stolen two years ago this month, by Juan Soto, who is now confined in the Tucson jail. The animals were found near Smithville." Tombstone Prospector, August 5, 1888: "Seventy-five caskets and coffins arrived at Fairbank yesterday, consigned to the well known undertaking establishment of Watt and Tarbell."

During 1888, Fairbank seemed to have more than it's share of crime, shootings, and stabbings.

One story of a Fairbank crime and a trial, were unusual to say the least.

A Chinese man had been jailed for stabbing and killing a fellow Chinese. The accused spoke only Chinese and understood not one word of English. It was extremely difficult to locate an interpreter who understood Chinese. Finally, a Mexican was found who spoke some Chinese. Court was in session and the judge asked the defendant if he had killed the Chinese man who had been stabbed. When the Mexican explained to the Chinaman what the judge had asked, the Chinese stood and delivered a fifteen minute dissertation -- in Chinese. The judge and jury looked expectantly at the interpreter, who replied, "He say no!" Case dismissed.

Lucero, fearless and honest, was Slaughter's most outstanding deputy. In fact, he and Burt Alvord were the sheriff's workhorses. Lucero walked right into the ambush that Frederico Acuna had prepared for John Slaughter. The hapless deputy never knew what hit him.

Lucero had gone down to the Mescal Ranch, which was just over the border in Mexico, and camped on the ranch. Little did he dream that Manuel Robles, who had sworn to revenge for the gun battle in French Joe Canyon, was watching his every move. Also camped in a nearby canyon were two other revenge minded Mexicans, Frederico Acuna and Geronimo Miranda.

On Sunday morning Lucero went down to the creek, which was about two hundred yards from the ranch house. He went unarmed and he should never have done such a thing. As he returned from the creek a rifle shot rang out, quickly followed by a second report. Lucero dropped in his tracks and did not move again.

Hands at the ranch said they saw two men ascertain that their victim was dead, then run away. They were recognized as Frederico Acuna and Geronimo Miranda, two of the train robbers.

When Lucero's body was examined it was found to have two bullet wounds through the head. Death had been instantaneous.

Unfortunately, Slaughter was never to capture or kill the men who ambushed his deputy, but fate measured out justice to at least two of them. Manuel Robles and Geronimo, both of whom were severely wounded by Sheriff Slaughter on separate occasions, joined forces in Mexico. They continued as outlaws and bushwhackers until both were shot to death by Mexican Rurales in the Sierra Madre Mountains.

Old time lawmen always claimed that John Slaughter provided a great deal of financial assistance to his murdered deputy's family.

In August, 1888, John Slaughter had an unusual experience while coming back to Tombstone from Fairbank. A crazy Italian woman was placed in his charge to be brought back to the county jail. The sheriff had a great deal of trouble getting her into the carriage. Finally, he told her that he would take her back to Italy if she got in. She did, but after about five miles of travel, the woman, who had been quiet, made a break and jumped out.

The sheriff and the driver finally got her back into the carriage, but she bit both of them several times during the process. The rest of the way to Tombstone they were obliged to hold her to prevent her from doing bodily harm to herself or them.

She was placed in the county jail until Judge Monk could examine her. When he did so, he ruled that no indication of insanity was found to exist and discharged her.

Miguel Chacon was a notorious horse thief well known in both Arizona and Sonora. In the summer of 1887, he stole a number of horses from Attorney Wilson's ranch on the San Pedro near Benson. He struck quickly in a surprise move and when he had control of the horses he stampeded them into Sonora. Nothing more was seen or heard of him until he ventured back into Tombstone on August 24, 1888.

When he arrived in town, he immediately went to a friend's house in the lower end of town. Very soon after his arrival Sheriff Slaughter was informed of his whereabouts. He was warned to be extremely cautious as Miguel was a "bad man", who would strongly resist any attempt that was made to deprive him of his freedom.

However, when the sheriff walked into the house alone where Chacon was hiding and told him to throw up his hands, he did so quickly and was soon lodged in jail.

Miguel Chacon was bound over to court on August 27, 1888, by Justice Shearer for stealing horses. He and his band of thieves had stolen 150 head of horses from Cochise County alone. They had stolen and sold all of Charley Hand's teams in Sonora; and, as a result, had bankrupted the poor man to where he had to go to work on the railroad.

By the fall of 1888, due to the efforts of Sheriff Slaughter, the leaders of this band of horse thieves were either serving their time in Yuma or awaiting trial in the county jail.

One of the times that Slaughter was embarrassed by the antics of Burt Alvord was in the early part of September, 1888. Burt and Fred Cardigan, both deputy sheriffs, met near Schmieding's Jewelry Store on Allen Street. They began to have an argument, the cause of which has never been known. Cardigan drew a pistol from his hip pocket and Alvord caught him by the arms and threw him to the boardwalk, falling on top of him. When they fell, Cardigan's pistol fired, the ball tearing a hole in the seat of his trousers, passing between his legs, and then through the leg of Alvord's trousers. The Chief of Police immediately arrested them and bound them over to Recorder Crowley.

Alvord was again involved in a mishap early in January, 1889. He was out on a skirmishing tour when a rabid dog insisted on trying to attack the horse he was riding. Drawing his six-gun, he made a motion with it just as his horse threw up his head. The pistol discharged, the ball hitting the horse's head. The horse fell and expired in a few minutes. Author's note: The report did not say what happened to the dog.

In January, 1889, the Tombstone Prospector carried an article concerning Geronimo Miranda and Sheriff Slaughter:

"Geronimo, murderer, train robber, horse thief, and probably the worst all around criminal outside bars, came within a hair's breadth of going across the divide last night or early this morning. Sheriff Slaughter had been on his trail since his escape after the train robbery in Sonora during which the trainmen were indiscriminately slaughtered about a year ago. The fight in the Whetstone Mountains in which part of the gang was killed by the sheriff's party; the ambushing and killing of one of Slaughter's most trusted deputies at the Mescal Ranch just below the line in old Mexico are just a few of the adventures in which this wily Mexican took a leading part.

"So bold and reckless had he become that he would enter this city at night and remain a day or two, even going so far at one time as to visit a saloon and play billiards until a friend warned him of the approach of his would be captors when he threw down his cue and darted out the back door.

"Yesterday, the sheriff was notified by one of his deputies that the man he wanted was in Charleston. Last night the sheriff determined to capture him and taking Deputy Sheriff Jesse Fischer with him, they proceeded to the town under the guidance of the man who had located the outlaw. Just at the right of the road near the bridge, which crossed the river at this point, is a tent and just behind the tent is a high board fence.

"The guide approached the opening in the tent and recognized the man lying asleep as Geronimo Miranda and returned with this information to the two officers. Slaughter held a ten bore shotgun similar to those carried by Wells Fargo & Co.'s messengers.

"Slaughter threw open the tent, entered and called to the man to get up. He jumped to his feet, recognized Slaughter, and quick as a flash, he bounded like a deer through the back of the tent, the sheriff after him. Before he could get his gun lined on the fleeing Geronimo, he was upon the fence. Quick as lightning, the sheriff lifted his gun and fired, and Geronimo fell off the other side. He picked himself up, however, and cut across to the other fence and was over this second impediment in a jiffy.

"Slaughter and his deputy were by this time around on the other side where the firing at the fleeing murderer was carried on, but he escaped in the bushes, and not a trace of him could be found.

"The entire charge of shot must have entered his body, for the blood could be seen on his shirt as the moon shone on him. Sheriff Slaughter says that the fellow was so quick that he had no opportunity to shoot until he poised for a moment on the fence. How badly he is wounded remains to be seen. Slaughter has worked indefatigably to bring this criminal to justice and no one will read this account of his escape without a feeling of regret that the sheriff's efforts were so near an accomplishment and that he could not have bagged his man."

Viola created a comical incident, while Slaughter was sheriff, (it was not comical to John). She was always afraid that one of John's guns would accidentally fire while she was in the midst of house cleaning. Because of that fear, she always unloaded his guns when she was cleaning.

Involved in closet cleaning one day, as usual, she unloaded John's pistol. Just after their dinner that night there was gunfire just three houses down Fremont Street from them. The sheriff grabbed his hat and his pistol and ran out the door on his way to the scene.

Just a few steps from his porch he realized that Viola was screaming to him. When he came back she told him that his pistol was unloaded. As John stuffed ammunition into his pistol, his only comment was, "I say, Vi, I say!"

This turned out to be another incident where Burt Alvord was an embarrassment to Sheriff Slaughter, although he was off duty when it occurred.

At about ten o'clock two pistol shots rang out at the house adjoining the corral on Second Street, just three doors east of Sheriff Slaughter's residence on Fremont Street.

Two men had been on the porch of the house, which was a frame building of two rooms. The gun flashes appeared to be toward City Hall. After the gunfire a man ran down to First Street, then disappeared in the direction of the hills south of town.

It all started with Deputy Sheriff Alvord, Wes Fuller, and two or three Mexicans, who were having an unusually good time at Fortino's house. Alvord had the only weapon there.

Fortino went out the front door and as he departed he picked up a hat and put it on his head. It was someone else's hat. Fuller seized the hat and Fortino objected. They began fighting over the hat. Fortino broke free and went out the door. Fuller seized Alvord's pistol and followed him out, fired two shots at him, one of them hitting Fortino in the side.

By the time any people arrived, Fortino, who was a brother of Fuller's wife, was lying on his front porch with a bullet hole in his left side. He had been dragged onto the porch by his aged mother.

It was later said that Fuller had been drinking heavily all day and that his wife had been trying to get him to go to bed. Fortino, who was a hard working man, had just come home from the Dragoon Mountains with a load of wood.

Alvord had either recovered his pistol or had acquired another. He and one of the Mexicans got into an argument and Alvord pulled his pistol on him. Mayor Thomas, who lived nearby, appeared on the scene and stopped the argument. Sheriff Slaughter, (with a loaded gun), and Deputy Cardigan arrived and that quieted all the belligerents. Bob Hatch, Ben Hyde, Cardigan and Slaughter left to locate Fuller; however, his friends had furnished him a horse and he was last seen in Fairbank early the next morning.

Dr. Dunn arrived to attend the wounded man, but there was nothing he could do. Fortino breathed his last about 1:00 A.M.

At the inquest, Alvord swore that Fortino was pounding him with a loaded black-snake whip before the shooting, knocking him down twice. Then Fortino assaulted Fuller with the whip and the latter shot him. Fuller had come into possession of the pistol by picking it up after Alvord had been knocked down and dropped it. Alvord stated that he had gone downtown after the shooting and got another pistol from Fred Lockling and had then gone back to the scene of the shooting.

On February 17, 1889, Wes Fuller came into Tombstone from his place of seclusion and surrendered to John Slaughter. He was in a terrible physical condition and could not lift a cup of water to his mouth, his nerves twitched so much. He claimed that there had been a free fight in progress and that he was justified in doing the killing.

In the early summer of 1880, a lithe, muscular man, wearing a long flowing moustache, a fringed buckskin jacket, and a matched pair of six-guns, rode into Tombstone. He was so well dressed that the casual observer might have taken him for a dude--but after a look into the cold blue eyes, and noting the worn handles on his guns, one knew that this was not so.

This man was Nashville Franklin Leslie, soon to be known as "Buckskin Frank". He was to stay in Tombstone for nine years and was to write his name indelibly in the town's bloody history. Leslie became one of Tombstone's best guns, it's most notorious ladies' man, and it's biggest liar.

That Wicked Little Gringo

He was described by those who knew him as good looking, of medium height, with regular features, an aquiline nose, blue eyes, and chestnut brown hair. Many of the old timers of Tombstone said that they believed Frank Leslie to be the most dangerous gunman ever to ride into Tombstone.

At a local dance one night Leslie became hopelessly captivated by a black haired beauty, named May Killeen. May had a husband named Mike. Although they were separated, Killeen made it known about town that he would shoot any man who showed her any attention. Leslie laughed and ignored such threats.

On June 22, 1880, Mike Killeen heard that Leslie and May were at a dance together. He went to the Cosmopolitan Hotel to wait for them. When the couple arrived arm in arm, Killeen rushed out to confront them. An argument ensued and guns began to roar. When they ceased, Mike Killeen was fatally wounded.

Frank was arrested and jailed until Killeen died. Since the dead man had publicly threatened to kill Leslie, no legal action was ever taken.

A few days after her husband had been conveniently planted in Boothill the comely widow married Frank Leslie. The new groom had difficulty adjusting to married life. He drank too much and he could not confine himself to one woman. The marriage was doomed.

On November 14, 1882, Billy Claibourne, known locally as "Billy the Kid", staggered into the Oriental Saloon considerably under the influence of whiskey. In the Oriental, he broke into Leslie's conversation with several other men and made insulting remarks to Frank. At first Leslie warned him, then as he grew more profane, he escorted him to the door and heaved him out.

A little later a man came into the Oriental and told Leslie that Claibourne was outside the front door with a rifle. He was bragging that he would kill Frank on sight. Several men had tried to talk him out of it, but he refused to be swayed.

Leslie went back into the Oriental and out through the double doors onto Fifth Street. When he was in shooting distance he leveled his pistol and called, "Come on, Billy, I don't want to kill you!"

Billy whirled and fired. Frank's pistol roared. The rifle bullet whistled by Frank. The pistol bullet struck Billy in the side, inflicting a fatal would.

The coroner's jury heard all of the evidence, then delivered the verdict that William Claibourne came to his death as the result of a pistol wound inflicted by Frank Leslie and that the shooting was in self defense and justifiable.

Once again Leslie went free because he had killed in self defense. Still, public opinion turned against him. Many local citizens thought that he was too quick with his gun. The Oriental began to lose customers because he was employed there. Milt Joyce, the owner, had to let him go.

Leslie went down to the Swisshelm Mountains to manage the Magnolia Ranch, which was also owned by Joyce. The ranch was nineteen miles from Tombstone and twenty miles from Mexico. Joyce moved to San Francisco in May,1885, and Leslie took over the ranch.

After seven years, May finally divorced Frank. She alleged that he had committed adultery with one of the "red light" girls, one Birdie Woods: that at times, he had beaten and choked her (May): that he failed to provide for her: and that he was frequently drunk.

Leslie did not defend the case.

The divorce was granted on September 3, 1887, and was signed by Judge William H. Barnes. It gave May a one-eighth share of the ranch and cattle, or $650 in cash. She received her freedom and Frank was ordered to pay her costs plus legal expenses to attorneys Herring & Herring.

After that, much of Leslie's time was spent in the Bird Cage Theatre with the girls from the red light district. One of the singers, a young girl, was a favorite of his. This blonde singer was Mollie Williams, who sometimes called herself Mollie Bradshaw.

Tombstone denizens called her Blonde Mollie. Billy King, an old time Tombstone saloon keeper, remembered her singing duets with Billy Hutchinson and that she had come to Tombstone from Nevada with E.L. Bradshaw.

She was a bosomy blonde and Leslie wanted her. The fact that she already had a boyfriend in fact, a hard case, who had already killed a man in Tombstone during an argument over a shirt--did not bother him at all.

Bradshaw turned up dead in a Tombstone alley one morning, a hole in his head. Many said that Leslie killed him in order to get Mollie. Frank did not admit that he did it, he didn't deny it either.

They buried Bradshaw in an unmarked grave in Boothill and Leslie took Blonde Mollie to the ranch in the Swisshelms to keep him company during the long nights. He also hired a young man, named James Neal, as a handy man about the ranch. Every night Blonde Mollie and Frank drank large quantities of raw liquor and the end result was always the same. Each night they would get into a violent quarrel.

For some reason Frank became insanely jealous of the smallest attention that Jim showed Mollie. On the evening of July 10, 1889, he rode in to find Mollie and Jim sitting on the front porch talking. Enraged, he drew his pistol. Mollie saw what he was about and fled around the house. Leslie's gun roared and the bullet struck Mollie in the head. When Frank saw that he had killed Mollie, he realized that he could not leave any witnesses to his crime. He turned his gun on Jim Neal and the muzzle spat flame and leaden death. Neal collapsed in a limp heap.

Sheriff John Slaughter dispatched officers to the Magnolia Ranch to arrest Leslie. Deputy Lawrence, Ben James, Billy King, and "Bloody Frank" Broad caught up with Leslie at the Four Bar Ranch and talked him into coming back to town with them. They did not tell him that Jim Neal was alive and had been brought into town by Dr. Goodfellow.

Frank had told the story that Neal had killed Mollie and then tried to kill him, so he had killed Neal in self defense. In the sheriff's office when he saw that Neal was still alive, he realized that he was caught and told the real story, admitting that he had killed Blonde Mollie.

On January 5, 1890, he pled guilty to the murder of Mollie Williams. On January 9, 1890 he was sentenced to life imprisonment in the Territorial Prison at Yuma.

Sheriff John Slaughter delivered Frank Leslie to the prison. He was entered as Convict #632, height five feet, seven inches, and weighing 135 pounds.

The Yuma Sentinel said that all the prisoners brought to Yuma were drunk. The Epitaph replied, "The Sentinel is in error and a simple denial by Mr. Slaughter is sufficient."

On the morning of January 26, 1890, a man named Sid Thomas, notified Sheriff Slaughter that a murder had been committed on the Duncan brothers' ranch in the west Huachuca Mountains.

The three Duncan brothers had a ranch that was near the Mexican boundary line. One of them, the one named David, had been paralyzed for about four years and totally unable to do any work. He had also been suffering from La Grippe and was confined to his bed on Saturday (25th). The other two brothers had left for their place of work that day, which was about three miles from the house.

When they returned that night they were met with a horrible sight. Lying on his back, in a pool of his own blood, their brother, David, was dead. It was evident that the entire house had been ransacked, and all their valuables were missing. Since everything of value had been taken from the house, it appeared that robbery had been the objective of the perpetrators. Rifles, pistols, a watch, and money had been among the items taken.

The unfortunate brother had been stabbed through the heart with a long knife, the blade passing entirely through his body. There was no evidence of a struggle and it appeared that he had been killed while he was asleep.

That Wicked Little Gringo

Sheriff Slaughter, City Coroner Hawke, and George W. Swain, left Tombstone and went to the scene of the butchery to hold an inquest immediately after receiving the news. The inquest revealed that David's body had a bullet wound in the lower part of the neck and two stab wounds in the breast.

Sheriff Slaughter put one of his most trusted deputies and a Mexican tracker on the trail which had been made by two horses. The tracks were very distinct and were made by one shod and one unshod animal.

This deputy and tracker returned to Tombstone after a fruitless quest. They followed the trail for four days, then lost it and could not find it again. They came upon the dead carcass of a cow that had been killed and partially skinned. The killers had cut a few ribs from the choicest part of the animal and cooked them, then moved on. The cow was of the Snake brand.

A local paper said of the crime: "Since the Apaches ceased their devilment there has not been a more cold-blooded, heartless murder than this."

Local feeling was that those who had committed the horrible crime would never be apprehended, as they had not been identified and were, by then, safely in Mexico.

The body of David Duncan was buried near the ranch house. A strange number of incidents and possibly three more murders were involved in the murder of David Duncan.

Ten years before, in 1880, two Cameron brothers purchased the San Raphael Land Grant west of the Huachuca Mountains. The grant ran all the way to the Mexican border. The brothers' family was politically powerful even in the federal government. The Camerons hired Julius Cundy as their ranch foreman and he hired a hard bitten crew of hands.

Since they had invested a great deal of money, the Camerons tried to dominate large portions of public domain and use it for free grazing. What they seemed to be unable to accept was that when land is filed upon by homesteaders, it is no longer open range.

The Camerons or their hired hands had already tried to run George McLane off his ranch which was located at Babocomari Creek, and tried the same with David de la Ossa at Lochiel.

Winfield Scott and Mary Fritz had a quarter section homestead in Bear Canyon on the west side of the Huachucas. James Rafferty lived with them, but he also had a quarter section of land. Joseph Raymond and Joseph McFarland lived together and they both held homestead papers. David Duncan and Charles Stewart held land that was about a mile from Bear Canyon. William and Thomas Duncan lived further on, but held homestead land. What these ten people had in common was that all of them had filed claim on land that the Camerons had intended for their use only.

Gossip in the hills said that Rafferty had been involved in the murder of a young Mexican boy, who delivered mescal to Bear Canyon customers.

Mary Fritz appeared to be a young woman living in fear. On one occasion she confided to Mr. John Hart that Rafferty had had nothing to do with the murder but that a Scotch man had. Her knowledge caused her death.

David Duncan was a county registrar, and as such, he traveled all over the county registering voters. He appeared at the Fritz house one night and while he was there he registered Winfield Fritz, J.E. McFarland, Merritt Sherman, James Rafferty, and Joseph Raymond. Duncan also stayed to eat dinner.

The next day three people from that house were found murdered. James Rafferty was found about a mile from the house, a bullet through the back of his head. Winfield Fritz had been shot down in his own doorway, apparently by someone he knew. Mary Fritz had been killed in her kitchen, shot thru her ear by a gun that was held so close that her hair was burned.

An inquest that lasted for two days was held at the Fritz home. Later several hearings were conducted in the courthouse in Tombstone. The Bear Canyon inquest was attended by about thirty people, among them Colin Cameron. Numerous questions were asked about the lynching of the Mexican boy, Antonio Quivernes. It was strange, but not one person present could verify that there had even been a lynching.

Cochise County Deputy John Franklin Jeffords arrested William Duncan and Charles Stewart at the scene of the crime. Likely, his reason for this was because they lived close by, but claimed that they had not heard any shots. They were held a short while then released.

William Duncan and John McFarland were then arrested and charged with murder on November 17, 1884. They were held without bail in the county jail. Lack of evidence against them caused the case to be dropped on May 18, 1885.

Charles Stewart, Thomas Duncan, and David Duncan were then arrested and jailed. They were held for six months, then released. While they were in jail, David came down with rheumatism. He was crippled for the rest of his life.

It now seemed that everyone but the killer or killers had been arrested. When David was killed on January 25, 1890, the other brothers knew quite well who the the man was who laid the plans and paid to have the deed done. All the people attending the Bear Canyon inquest had known who the killer of Rafferty and the Fritzes were. The killer had sat there among them....and they knew who had had David Duncan killed too. But knowing who the killer was, and having sufficient evidence to prove it, were two different things.

In February, 1890, Sheriff Slaughter brought Chinaman Sam Hing Ching into district court where testimony was heard, both for the defense and the prosecution. The defendant, who had pled guilty to murder, was sentenced to the Territorial Prison at Yuma for the rest of his natural life.

Reporters are in a class unto themselves:

"Three of the colored troops, who fought at the "Battle of Wham Run" last summer have been presented with medals by the department for bravery while in action. The medals for the other side have not been cast yet." Daily Prospector, February 24, 1890.

"Another capture has been credited to Sheriff Slaughter. He has caught Jesus Navarro burglarizing a house, with a saddle and other articles in his possession."

On April 11, 1890, John Slaughter received word from Bisbee that Constable William Lowther had been killed by James Daly. Slaughter hurried to Montgomery's O.K. Corral, took a buckboard and team, and set out for Bisbee.

Before he left Tombstone he had sent a deputy to the customs house to alert the guards there to be on the lookout for the fugitive who might be trying to cross the border.

Slaughter arrived in Bisbee a few hours later to find the entire town excited and buzzing. Everyone wanted to tell him what had happened, so it took a while for him to get an accurate account. Daly had beaten a Mexican a short time before and the victim had sworn out a warrant for his arrest. Lowther had gone to make the arrest, refusing the offer of Deputy Sheriff Bell to accompany him.

Lowther rode down to Daly's home which was roughly a mile below town. He tied his horse to a tree and walked toward the house which was enclosed by a pole fence. When he went through the gate Daly came out his front door, leveled a double barreled shotgun, and from the distance of but a few feet, emptied it's contents at the lawman. The first barrel blew away a portion of Lowther's coat, the second blew a very large hole in his chest. The milkman, on his rounds, found the body and notified the authorities.

Daly was seen running toward the hills behind his house immediately after the shooting and no one had seen anything of him since.

A reward was quickly offered and grew to $2,500, offered by the Copper Queen Mining Company and the citizens of Bisbee, plus another $500 was offered by John Slaughter and the County Board of Supervisors.

Several parties on foot and on horseback searched the countryside and riders were dispatched to outlying ranches as

That Wicked Little Gringo

well as along the border to warn people about the murderer. Whether Daly was mounted, or on foot, was not known for sure. Many local people believed that he had deliberately planned the murder, but had expected to see Slaughter appear with the warrant, not Lowther. At a later date, it was discovered that he had had a horse nearby, ready to carry him across the border into Mexico when his dastardly deed had been accomplished.

Lowther had been well liked by everyone. He had been a extremely quiet man, who never sought trouble. When his body was examined, the warrant he had come to serve was still in his pocket and his pistol still in it's holster.

James Daly was described as a man who appeared to be about fifty years of age, but he was actually several years younger. He was five feet, ten inches tall, had a round face, a sandy moustache, and weighed about 165 pounds. Several people, who knew him, said that they had heard him say many times that he would never be arrested again. They also knew him to be always armed, no matter the occasion.

Many believed that Daly would be arrested and taken into Tombstone under cover of darkness and locked in the county jail. That way he would be safe from a large number of indignant and outraged citizens.

Daly had many friends among the Mexican people and it was sure that they would confuse the officers as much as possible. It was doubtful that Daly would ever have been hanged for killing Lowther, as no one could disprove any reasonable story that he told regarding the shooting.

Lowther was a highly respected man and member of the Masonic Lodge, under whose auspices his funeral was held.

Chief of Police Gage arrested Thomas Forget while he was in the act of purloining ore from the Northwest mine, which belonged to the Tombstone Mill & Mining Company.

When Forget was being examined by Judge Easton, a coat was brought into the court. It was a long, heavy one with large, canvas pockets on the inside, where he had carried the ore found upon him when he was arrested. The pockets were capable of containing at least fifty pounds of ore each without being noticeable. Seven sacks of very rich ore had been found in his cabin, they had been confiscated and conveyed to the justice's courtroom. This ore had been taken from the sorted pile on the dump at the Northwest shaft.

Forget escaped from the county jail in May, 1890. This was the first escape from the jail during John Slaughter's term of office. He was quite upset by such an event and offered a $200 reward for the return of the escaped prisoner.

A comment by the Prospector was worth noting: "Nothing has thus far been heard of Tom Forget. He will soon be Tom Forgotten."

Slaughter had received word that Forget had been captured on the morning of September 13, 1890, in Separ. Forget had attended a horse race and had just bet $10, when he walked right into the arms of a deputy sheriff who had been searching for him.

When he arrived back in Tombstone he explained to John Slaughter how he had escaped his jail. He had simply climbed over the jail wall and dropped into the alley running behind the courthouse. He had dodged several men who were looking for him, some of them coming within a few feet of him. Forget said that he had walked to Contention and after a rest had gone on to Benson. Still walking, he had gone into the Whetstone Mountains where he had stayed for eight days.

Eleven days after he had escaped, he had returned to Tombstone and stayed there two days and two nights. While coming up Toughnut Street he had met the local banker and a lady on horseback, but they had not recognized him.

He had returned to Benson, then walked from there to Deming, New Mexico (160 miles). A rancher there had hired him to dig a well and erect a windmill. That job had taken him a month. When he had returned to Deming the first person he had seen was a woman from Tombstone, and she had recognized him.

That Wicked Little Gringo

A man named Fitzgerald, had given him a job at the American Mine, located at Hachita, where he had worked for forty days. Then another miner came there who had worked with him at the Grand Central Mine in Tombstone.

He had decided to move to Separ and while he was on the way there, four men had tried to rob him. They had not succeeded, but they had marked his face considerably in the attempt.

In Separ, he claimed that when he had seen Deputy Howell at the race track, he had given the deputy $60 to hold for him, and had come back with the deputy without waiting for extradition papers. The story about his bet on the horse race was true and he had won $15.

Lawmen, who had been at Separ, told a slightly different account. They said that Forget had been trying to catch a freight train, because he had known that they were after him and that he came very near to getting away. They had knocked him down just as he reached the train.

When Forget appeared in court, he pled not guilty, but a misdemeanor indictment was found against him for breaking jail.

The Territory vs. Forget was a trial by jury. John Gray, D. Huddy, W.F. Staunton, G.S. Reitstreake, Mike Welsh, John Slaughter, and Martin Welsh were examined for the prosecution. Argument, was heard by English and Staehle for the defense, and Colonel Herring for the prosecution. The defense offered no testimony.

After a one hour deliberation the jury found a verdict of guilty of of petty larceny.

In June, 1890, Burt Alvord demonstrated that he did have a sense of humor. He and Matt Burts were in Bisbee. When they decided to go home, they sent a telegram to the editor of the Tombstone Epitaph. It stated: "Bodies of Burts and Alvord will arrive this afternoon."

The editor spread the word and in no time at all, wild rumors abounded: the two men had been shot and killed, they had been stabbed, they had shot each other, and, they were dead from some unknown cause.

When the afternoon stage arrived in Tombstone, it was met by an Epitaph reporter and a majority of the local citizens. They expected to see it accompanied by a wagon carrying two coffins.

There were no coffins, but hale and hearty, Burts and Alvord climbed off the stage with huge grins.

"Well, our bodies arrived in Tombstone", they laughed, "we never go anywhere without them!"

The Epitaph sarcastically remarked in the next issue, "Maybe they will be old enough to quit acting like boys when Gabriel blows his horn."

When John Slaughter left the office of sheriff, Cochise County was more law abiding than at any time in its history. The thieves and killers had been killed, jailed, or scattered, and John felt that he could return to his ranch and concentrate on his cattle.

Slaughter's party and its leaders insisted that he continue as sheriff for one more term. They were planning to draft him when Viola said, "NO!" She said, "his business and his family need him, and we don't feel that he would live through another term." The attempt to draft John was dropped.

Although Viola admitted that John liked being sheriff even more than running his ranch, she had always dreaded the duties that took her husband away from Tombstone for days at a time. He was usually on the trail of some desperate man and she spent many sleepless nights wondering and fearful for the safety of her husband.

BADMEN ENCOUNTERED BY JOHN SLAUGHTER

Ed Lyle	Frederico Acuna
Cap Stillwell	Eduardo Moreno
Larry Sheehan	Augustin Chaeon
William Hughes	Geronimo Baltierrez
J.T. Blunt	Librado Marrojo
Dick Johnson	Pegleg Finney
Joseph Brooks	Carmen Mendibles
Jose Lopez aka Juan	Little Bob Stephens
Juan Soto	Nieves Deron
George Cleveland	Reilly Dutton
William Pallet'	Curly Bill Brocius
Guadalupe Robles	James Daly
Geronimo Miranda	Van Wyck Coster
Manuel Robles	Miguel Chacon

Newspaper Clippings, *circa 1887*

John Horton Slaughter

The town of Fairbank, Arizona, A.T.
as it looked during John Slaughter's time as sheriff.

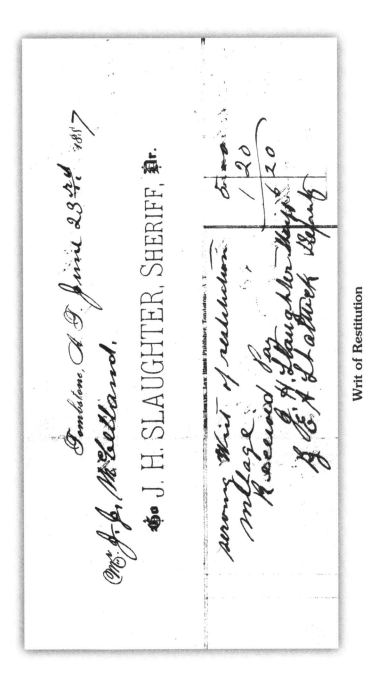

Writ of Restitution

— *Courtesy of Talei Publishers via Richard & Irise Lapidus*

AFFIDAVIT OF WITNESS.

CASE OF John H Slaughter

INDIAN DEPREDATIONS.

STATE OF Arizona
COUNTY OF Cochise

On this 3 day of July 18 18, before me Mr H Daily Clk Dist Court in and for said County and State personally appeared T A Rowland and Thomas Cochran to me well known, who being by me duly sworn according to law depose and say as touching the claim of John H Slaughter for losses sustained by reason of Indian depredations. That they are residents of Cochise and have been for the last 4 years. That they are personally well acquainted with the claimant John H Slaughter and have been for the last 4 years. That their Post-Office address is Tombstone Arizona That on or about the 5' day of June 1866, they were living at the ranch (San Bernardino) of Claimant and were engaged in the care of herding and guarding the cattle of Claimant That at that time the Indians generally recognized as of the Apache tribe were raiding through that section of the country, stealing or destroying property belonging to the settlers. That at that time said Indians stole 250 head of Cattle from Claimant John H Slaughter and drove them into Sonora Mexico – Four or five were killed on the ranch. The stealing was done at night and in full view of us – The next day we followed them into Sonora Mex – picked up 2 Indian mules (Ears split)

(OVER.)

Affidavit of John Slaughter
Indian Depredations - Side 1
John Slaughter testifies about Apache Indians stealing his cattle

That we know the facts from the following reasons: (Be careful to give reasons) — It was at Night
(Moonlight Night & we saw them drive
them away —

That said stock was well worth at that time (give values of each kind and variety of stock separately) — Four
Thousand dollars —

That we were familiar with the stock of said claimant, and would recognize it whenever we would see it. That after said raid none of said stock was ever seen about the neighborhood. That at the time of said loss the claimant was using the ordinary caution and care in looking after his stock. That these Indian raids were frequent and the settlers unable to prevent them, nor were they, as a rule, numerous enough to pursue the Indians with any prospect of success. That the Indians were a terror to the settlers, most of whom suffered loss of property, and many of them loss of life at their hands. That during this raid when this loss occurred many ranchmen lost cattle in part of the count. T. Eis. Cattle Company —

Said affiants further swear that they have no interest in the claim of said John H Slaughter
and that they are citizens of the United States.

WITNESS TO SIGNATURE:
James B Henry   T A Rowland
                   Thos X Cochrane
                        his

Subscribed and sworn to before me the day and year above written, after the contents of the affidavit were read over and explained to them, and I certify that these affiants are reputable men in this community, and their statements worthy of credit. Witness my hand and seal of office.

                    Geo H Daily
                    Clk Dist Court

Indian Depredations.
Dep't of Arizona
Claim of John H Slaughter

AFFIDAVIT OF WITNESS.

ISAAC R. HITT,
ATTORNEY,
CHICAGO, · · ILL.

Affidavit of John Slaughter
Indian Depredations - Side 2

DESCRIBE BUT ONE LOSS, BY ONE RAID, ON THIS BLANK.

INDIAN DEPREDATION CIRCULAR.

The answer should be written under the questions and then signed, and this paper mailed to us, when the proper papers will be prepared and sent to claimants and their witnesses for execution.

ISAAC R. HITT & CO., Chicago, Ills.,

Question 1. What is your name, age, occupation, and present P. O. address?

Answer. John H Slaughter 42 Rancher Tombstone

" 2. What number of cattle, horses, or sheep were stolen and what property destroyed? Give description of each and full particulars. In describing stock, give age, breed and brand. If a horse, sound or not sound, and if stock is put in at a high price, the particular qualities increasing price must be given.

Answer. 250 head of Cattle

" 3. Where did this raid take place, and when was it? Give day, month and year, if in daytime or at night, and name of County and State. Was said stock or property on said Indians' reservation at time stolen?

Answer. On Jany 3 1886 at night, at my ranch San Bernardino Cochise Co A.T.

" 4. Have you lost, hay, grain, buildings of any kind, fences, hedges or any kind of property whatsoever, by said Indians?

Answer.

" 5. What was the value in cash of the stock at that time per head? What was the value of other property taken or destroyed? If both stock and beef cattle, the number and val. no separately.

Answer. $3000 - all told or about $12 per head

" 6. Was stock in an enclosure or on open range and properly guarded?

Answer. Open Range properly guarded

" 7. To what tribe of Indians did these raiders belong? How do you know this?

Answer. Apache

" 8. Was any of the stock killed? Give particulars; were any Indian ponies picked up on the trail?

Answer. Some 4 or 5 head killed, balance driven away

" 9. Who saw the Indians commit the theft? What is their P. O. address?

Answer. F A Rowland Thos Coran P.O. Tombstone pursued into Sonora Mexico

" 10. Were the Indians pursued? and how far? and by whom, and their P. O. address?

Answer.

" 11. Was any of the property recovered? Give particulars.

Answer. No - 2 mules belonging to Indians were picked up which I still have in my possession

" 12. In the pursuit was there a fight; who was killed or wounded in that raid; State all particulars.

Answer. No fight -

Question Blank - Indian Depredations - *Side 1*
*Questionaire filled out by John Slaughter
regarding the stealing of his cattle by the Apache Indians*

Sheriff of Cochise 1887-1890

13. Who are your witnesses, what is their P. O. address, and were they neighbors or employees, and how do they know the facts? How do your witnesses know that you lost the property you claim to have lost at the time stated by you; and how do they know that the Indians belong to the tribe stated by you.

Answer T. A. Borland & Wm Corons Tombstone employees saw them take the cattle

14. What neighbors lost horses or cattle by same Indians in same raid? Give P. O. address of each.

Answer Erie Cattle Co and Sansomo Cattle & Cow Cattle — P.O. Tombstone

15. Did you ever receive any pay, on account of said loss?

Answer No sir, this is my first application

16. Did you ever apply to any one for pay, and whom and when?

Answer No

17. Do you know anything more about this loss not already stated?

Answer Nothing but minor incidents

18. Was father, mother, brother or sister, killed, wounded or ravished, by said Indians, state all particulars; and if there is not room in this blank, send particulars by letter to us, give age of victim at time, married or not married?

Answer

Copy

ISAAC R. HITT & Co. and John W. Bailey are authorized to collect this claim for a fee of 50 per cent. with the understanding that no fee will be charged if nothing is collected.

Sign here John H Slaughter

Answer these questions as far as you can on every loss you suffered on any one Indian raid.

INDIAN DEPREDATIONS.
QUESTION BLANK.
State of Arizona
Claim of John H Slaughter
ISAAC R. HITT & CO.,
ATTORNEYS
CHICAGO, ILL.

Question Blank - Indian Depredations - Side 2

That Wicked Little Gringo

Juan Soto
Outlaw and badman left for parts unknown at Slaughter's suggestion.

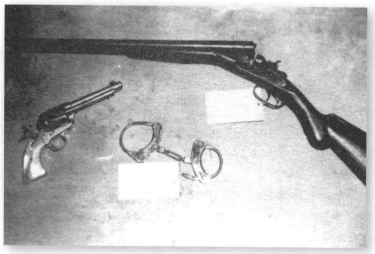

Weapons used by John Slaughter

MURDERED FOR HIS MONEY.

An American Foully Murdered In Sonora.

September 8, 1888.

Information was received at the Epitaph office this morning to the effect that last Sunday or Monday, Charles Jones, a former resident of this place, was brutally murdered near Santa Anna, in the State of Sonora. This is a small Mexican town on the A. & N. M. road, about twenty miles from Magdalena, to which place his body was taken and buried. He left here about two weeks ago intending to go to Altar for the purpose of purchasing a band of horses. He was evidently waylaid and murdered for his money and possessions, as his wounds, three in number, were from a rifle, all showing that he was shot from behind. His money, horse, arms and equipments, and most of his clothes were taken by the assassins. He formerly worked for John H. Slaughter, and also worked hauling wood for Mr. Johnson of Bisbee. He was a very industrious, hard-working man, and was highly esteemed by those who knew him. It is not known whether he has any relations in this country or not, but it is believed he has in Missouri, where he owned considerable landed property. No clue has yet been found as to who committed the deed.

Report on the brutal murder of Charles Jones
A former employee of John Slaughter

$1,000 REWARD.

The above reward will be paid for the arrest and detention in any jail in the United States or in the Republic of Mexico, of Albert Alvord and Wm. Stiles, who broke jail in Tombstone on the night of December 15. 1903.

The above reward will be paid for the arrest of both, or $500 for either man. The reward is good for one year. Wire at my expense.

A. V LEWIS,
Sheriff of Cochise County.
Tombstone, Ariz., Jan. 2, 1904.

$200 REWARD,

I will pay the above reward for the return of

THOMAS FORGET,

Who escaped from the Cochise County jail on the evening of May 7th, 1890.

Description.—He is a man about 5 feet six inches high, a French Canadian 42 years of age; talks broken English, wears moustache and sideburns, dark complection, had on pair of shoes.

JOHN SLAUGHTER,
Sheriff Cochise County.

REWARD NOTICES

Prospector
February 4, 1890

The funeral of the late Alfred Richards was largely attended this afternoon by the friends of the deceased. The Tombstone band lead the solemn procession as it wended its way to the cemetery. The occasion was one of more than an ordinary nature. The manner in which the deceased met his death and his sudden separation from his friends created a feeling in the breasts of those who even had not known him personally, that they were interested in seeing the being who had caused his untimely taking off, speedily pay the penalty for his awful crime.

< Funeral Notice
Al Richards

RICHARDS' DEATH.

He Dies Sunday Morning Without Regaining His Reason.

February 3, 1890.

The horrible crime committed in the heart of the city by which Al Richards met an untimely death at the hands of a midnight assassin is still the topic of conversation in all circles. In the history of this city no crime was ever committed, so atrocious and cold blooded in its nature. As mentioned in Saturday's Epitaph Drs. Goodfellow and Huse performed the operation of raising the skull off the brain of the unconscious victim, in the hope that he would rally and at least be able to talk and tell something that could be used as a clue to ferret out the assassin. The operation was successfully performed, and although the most careful nursing and attendance was given him, he breathed his last twelve hours after the operation was performed, without uttering a word. As he breathed his last he attempted to say something, but the sentence died before he had completed it and was unintelligible.

Little knots of people gathered around the scene of the crime and discussed the probability of ever discovering the murderer. Various rumors were afloat, and two or three parties were placed under arrest but released after becoming convinced that they could not have been implicated.

The body was removed to the undertaking rooms of Watt & Tarbell, where Dr. Goodfellow examined the head of the deceased. After the scalp was removed it was evident that the blow that caused the death of Richards was dealt with the blunt end of the axe, as stated in the Epitaph. The blow must have been a terrible one, and given with the intent to kill on the spot. The entire skull was cracked, and the scar on the forehead was but a slight evidence of the deadly work. All over the top and back of the head the skull was cracked open in many places, while the wound in the forehead fitted the blunt end of the axe that had been found by the bedside of the murdered man.

C. S. Fly photographed the head after the scalp had been removed, and nothing has been or will be left undone by the friends of the deceased to bring to justice the perpetrator of the most diabolical murder ever committed in Tombstone.

Report on the assassination of Al Richards

REWARD NOTICES

$500 Reward.

In accordance with a resolution passed by the Board of Supervisors Feb. 10, 1890. I hereby offer a reward of Five Hundred Dollars for the arrest and conviction of the murderer or murderers of DAVID D. DUNCAN, who was killed in the Huachuca mountains on or about January 25th, 1890.

JOHN H. SLAUGHTER, Sheriff.

Dated Tombstone, Feb. 11, 1890.

$500 Reward.

In accordance with a resolution passed by the Board of Supervisors Feb 10, 1890. I hereby offer a reward of Five Hundred Dollars for the arrest and conviction of the murderer or murderers of ALFRED RICHARDS, who was killed in Tombstone, Cochise county, Arizona, on the night of January 31st, 1890.

JOHN H. SLAUGHTER, Sheriff.

Dated Tombstone, Feb. 11, 1890.

No. 185

In the matter of the inquest held on the body of

Year 1890 — Alfred Richards, Deceased.

Inquest held by I. C. Easton, J.P., Coroner.

		PROCEEDINGS.	DR.	CR.
Feb.	2	Inquest held.		
Mch.	4	Filed,		
		Cause of death, blow on the head, by a blunt instrument on the night of Friday Jan. 31st/890 by a person or persons unknown. Age 48 years. Native of Cornwall, England, died Feb 2d 1890.		

Notice of Inquest — *Death of Al Richards*

No. 177

In the matter of the inquest held on the body of

Year 1888 — Guadalupe Robles, Deceased.

Inquest held by W. D. Shearer, Coroner.

		PROCEEDINGS.	DR.	CR.
June	7	Inquest held		
Jan	17	Filed		
		Cause of death, "gun shot wounds".		

Notice of Inquest — *Death of Guadalupe Robles*

Burt Alvord — *A lawman turned outlaw*

— **Jeff Miltons's house** —
Still standing at the corner of Third & Safford streets

TERRITORIAL PRISON AT YUMA, A. T.
DESCRIPTION OF CONVICT

Name: Albert Alvord   Number: 2064
Alias: Sentence: 2 yrs. from 12/8/1903
Crime: Attempt to rob U.S. Mail   Nativity: California
County: Cochise   Age: 40
Legitimate Occupation: Cowman
Habits: Intemperate   Tabacco: Yes
Opium: No   Religion: Catholic
Size of Head: 7 1/8   Size of Foot: 8
Height: Weight:
Color of Eyes: Gray   Color of Hair: Brown
Married: Divorced   Children:
Living Relatives:
Can Read: Yes   Can Write: Yes
Where Educated: Self-educated   Former Imprisonment:

When and How Discharged: Oct. 9, 1905 Expiration of sentence
Article from book - "Capt. Mossman"
Gave Sheriff Lewis a woven horse hair belt, trimmed with silver buckles m.
from Mexican dollars

PRISON RECORD

AZ Daily Citizen - 12-15-1900
Graham Guardian - 5-10-1901, 9-4-1903, 12-18-1903, 1-1-1904
AZ Silver Belt - 2-18-1904, 2-23-1904, 9-18-1904
AZ Sentinel - 2-26-1902, 9-17-1902, 7-15-1903, 12-9-1903
AZ Silver Belt - 9-1-1904
AZ Sent. - 2-17-1904, 2-24-1904, 3-9-1904
Tombstone Epitaph - 9-15-1907
AZ Sent - 10-18-1905, 7-17-1907
The Copper Era - Dec. 5, 1901, Sept. 25, 1902

— Albert Alvord's prison description —

Matt Burts — Yuma Penitentiary photograph

— Augustine Chacon - 1902 —
Chacon and Slaughter were bitter enemies.

Sources:

Prospector	April 9, 1887
Ibid	April 13, 14, 1887
Ibid	December 2, 1887
Daily Prospector	May 9, 1887
Prospector	August 12, 1887
Ibid	November 18, 1887
Ibid	November 22, 1887
Ibid	August 30, 1887
Ibid	September 2, 1887
Ibid	February 28, 1888
Ibid	February 29, 1888
Ibid	March 11, 1888
Ibid	May 12, 1888
Ibid	June 9, 188S
Daily Prospector	July 18, 1888
Ibid	August 3, 1888
Ibid	August 17, 1888
Ibid	August 24, 1888
Ibid	August 26, 1888
Epitaph	August 25, 1888
Ibid	August 28, 1888
Ibid	September 13, 1888
Ibid	January 6, 1889
Prospector	January 12, 1889
Ibid	January 27, 1889
Daily Prospector	February 15, 1889
Ibid	February 16, 1889
Ibid	February 18, 1889
Prospector	January 28, 1889
Epitaph	July 11, 1889
Prospector	July 12, 1889
Daily Prospector	July 15, 1889
Ibid	December 16, 1889
Epitaph	January 6, 1890
Ibid	January 11, 1890
Ibid	January 18, 1890
Daily Prospector	February 20, 1890
Ibid	February 24, 1890
Ibid	February 25, 1890
Ibid	April 12, 1890
Ibid	April 18, 1890
Ibid	April 15, 1890
Ibid	April 16, 1890
Ibid	May 8, 1890
Ibid	May 9, 1890
Ibid	June 10, 1890
Ibid	September 13, 1890
Ibid	September 15, 1890
Prospector	September 17, 1890
Ibid	September 19, 1890
Epitaph	June 10, 1890
Bisbee Daily Review	April 22, 1934

JOHN SLAUGHTER'S PLACE

Friends of Tad Rowland told John Slaughter that the San Bernardino land grant was for sale, and Senor Guillermo Andrade of Guaymas was acting as agent.

This old Mexican land grant was several thousand acres located in the extreme southeast corner of Arizona and extending south into Sonora. John and Viola acquired this vast range without seeing it.

They acquired the land from the three owners--one of them a descendant of the original owner. The two others were people who had bought from the descendants of the original owner, Ignacio Perez.

The Slaughters signed a ninety-nine year lease on 65,000 acres, one-third in Cochise, and two-thirds in Sonora, Mexico. That was roughly $1.25 an acre. The grant had flowing streams, artesian springs, and grass that was stirrup high. It had been deserted for fifty years.

The grant was first made to Perez in March, 1822. It was made and recorded in Arispe. It consisted of four sitios de ganado mayor. The grant originally consisted of 29,644 hectares, which is about 73,240 acres. When the original grant was given, it lay entirely in Mexico. Following the Gadsden Purchase, the international boundary was reestablished and a portion of the ranch was placed in the United States. When Slaughter acquired it in 1884, the border divided it into two unequal sized parts--the larger portion being in Mexico.

Title to the Perez grant was confirmed by the Court of Private Land Claims on February 10, 1900. It was surveyed by the U.S. Government on June, 13, 1902, and declared to be in Township 24, South, Ranges 30 and 31, east of the Gila and Salt River meridian. It contained 2,382 acres. The grant was patented by the United States on May 22, 1913.

Viola, in later years, told of their first sight of their new ranch, "As we came out of the Sulphur Springs Valley into a pass in the Silver Creek range, we looked east and south to the Guadalupes in New Mexico and into the distant blue of old Mexico. Two streams watered the valley. It was beautiful and it was ours."

The Slaughters did not move to the ranch for several years. Their first buildings were built close to the hacienda ruins by the Mexican border and near the large springs. Two adobe houses were built at first, one for John's in-laws to live in, and another for his foreman and cowhands. Viola kept a home in Tombstone in order that John's children and her brother, Jimmy could attend school.

Amazon and Mary Ann with their son, Stonewall, and John's foreman, all lived on the ranch taking care of it and hiring employees as needed. John went back and forth between Tombstone and the ranch, busy buying and selling cattle, and running his meat market business.

A major earthquake shook most of southeast Arizona and a good part of Sonora in 1887. It was said to be of a magnitude of 7.2 and caused major destruction of property, fifty-one deaths, and numerous injuries in Mexico. The small town of Bavispe was the epicenter of the quake and the activity diameter extended 300 miles.

This quake rocked an area of 720,000 square miles and caused a thirty-five mile long scarp with an offset of fourteen feet. Ground water disturbances caused many springs and wells to go dry. Rock falls in the Mule, Dragoon, Whetstone, Huachuca, Swisshelm, Pedregosa, and Dos Cabeza Mountains caused many brush fires from sparks.

Both the adobe houses, the smoke house, the milk house, and the stables on Slaughter's ranch were totally destroyed.

Amazon Howell barely escaped being crushed as the entire adobe house collapsed around him. Seven thousand adobe blocks had been used in building the two main houses. Only 120 of them were not broken in the quake.

When the quake struck, Viola had been visiting at Contention Hill, and John had been in the Tombstone courthouse. Neither of them were injured, and the damage sustained by Tombstone was minimal.

Following the earthquake, the Howells moved to Tombstone and lived there the rest of Amazon's life. Stonewall died of pneumonia on October 22, 1889, just one day before his twenty-sixth birthday. Amazon died on August 29, 1890. Both are buried in the Tombstone City Cemetery.

The Territorial Governor issued a quarantine proclamation against Mexican cattle in 1887. It stated that Mexican cattle could be imported, but they first had to be held at the border for ninety days, then inspected before they were brought into Arizona. John Slaughter was always quick to take advantage of any situation. He built a quarantine fence that enclosed his property north of the border. Up until then, all the area had been used as open range. When this fence was built it fenced in a large number of cattle that belonged to other ranchers. When the quarantine was lifted John loosed all the cattle wearing brands. During the quarantine period many of the cows had had calves. John released all of the calves that he did not own, but not until they had been marked with his "Z" brand.

Another isolation period was declared in 1897. This time Slaughter, the Ryan brothers, and the Erie Cattle Company ordered 280,000 pounds of barbed wire and 6,000 posts. They built a four strand, fifty mile long drift fence. It ran from a point five miles south of Bisbee along the border to connect with a twenty-five mile stretch of fence built in 1890 by the San Simon Cattle Company. This construction provided a seventy-five mile long continuous fence along the border.

This fence stood until 1903, at which time the Bureau of the Interior ordered its destruction. All the owners, except

That Wicked Little Gringo

Slaughter, complied with the order. For some unknown reason John refused to tear down his section of fence. Eventually, the Bureau sued him, and finally, in April, 1910, he began to tear it down.

Addie Slaughter attended school in Tombstone during that town's wildest years. When she was eighteen years old John sent her to Field's Seminary in Oakland, California. It was a fashionable school for young ladies and Addie spent two years there, graduating with a gold medal.

Following graduation, Addie moved back to the San Bernardino and became a secretary for her father. She answered his correspondence, assumed responsibility for the ranch payroll and kept the buying and selling cattle records.

On one occasion, the Smithsonian Institute sent an ornithologist to collect information on birds of the San Bernardino. John Slaughter liked the young man and called him "Hondoo". Before long, everyone did as well. Addie acted as his guide on his field trips around the ranch. Hondoo was very good with firearms and had brought his guns with him to the wild west. During their outings he taught Addie to shoot. She became an excellent marks woman, and one day on an impulse, she shot his hat off.

When Addie was thirty years old she met a young doctor from Rhode Island. His name was Dr. William Arnold Greene. He was thirty-four.

The couple were married September 9, 1903, in the Roy Hotel parlor. Theirs was the first Episcopal marriage in Douglas. The newlyweds moved to Chicago, but after a year they came back to Douglas and bought a home at 825 Ninth Street. All three of their children were born in this home: John Slaughter in 1905, William Arnold Jr. in 1907, and Adeline Howell in 1911.

Dr. Greene was a respected doctor and member of the community. He was a member of the Masonic and Elks lodges, and the first president of the Kiwanis Club. He even found time to serve as Douglas' mayor from 1908-1910. During the revolution along the border, both the American and Mexican governments praised him. He died on December 15, 1924.

After her daughter married in 1939, Addie moved in with Viola. She suffered a heart attack and died on February 28, 1941, just three weeks before Viola died on April 1, 1941.

In 1895, Jimmy Howell had built a home for he and Mary Ann about a mile from the ranch house. John Slaughter had sent Jimmy to St. Matthew's Military Academy in San Mateo, California, then to General City Business College in Quincy, Illinois.

Jimmy spoke Spanish fluently and was an excellent bookkeeper. While he kept books for the ranch, he also ran his own cattle on the San Bernardino and supplied beef to the construction crews that built the El Paso & Southwestern Railroad.

At one time he held the position of Cochise County Roads supervisor and was later elected to the Twenty-second Territorial Assembly from Cochise County.

Jimmy continued to live on the ranch with his mother and did not marry until 1903, when he was past thirty years of age.

Jimmy was injured by a bucking horse and had to spend some time in the hospital. Not long after, he married his nurse, Frances (Frankie) Todd on April 28, 1903.

Shortly after their marriage, Mary Ann moved in with Viola and John, living there the rest of her life.

The newlyweds lived in Tombstone and Bisbee, moving to Douglas in 1909. Jimmy was active in the Knights of Pythias, Elks, and Kiwanis.

After a long illness, he died in Douglas on January 24, 1936, and is buried at the Douglas Calvary Cemetery.

Mary Ann, was known to everyone as Grandma Howell. She lived another thirty years after Amazon died, passing away on the San Bernardino ranch on April 9, 1920. She is buried in the Tombstone City Cemetery between her son, Stonewall, and her husband, Amazon.

That Wicked Little Gringo

In 1892, after serving two terms as sheriff, John was having a hard time making the ranch pay. Viola finally said, "Mr. Slaughter, we will give up this Tombstone house, and we will all go to the ranch and help out. All I want is a plain house with board floors, muslin ceilings and board finishes around the adobes."

Viola had her way, and the Slaughters moved to the San Bernardino, into a three room adobe building that later became the ranch schoolhouse.

The ranch house was probably completed in the late spring or early summer of 1893. It contained six rooms, three on each side of a long hall, which had been in the original structure. At a later date, a kitchen, a bath, a cowboy dining room, and a family combination living-dining room were added. An adobe commissary was built about the same time as the house. A wooden bunk house for the hands, a chicken house, and a barn were included in the ranch buildings. Around 1900 an ice house, a wash house, and a granary were added.

The fact that John and Viola both were Southern folk was reflected in the construction of their ranch house which had verandas and hipped roofs.

One of the buildings on the ranch near Boundary Monument No. 77, was constructed so that half of it lay in Mexico and the other half in the United States. When U.S. Deputy Surveyor John A. Rockfellow ran the San Bernardino land grant boundaries on July 19, 1901, he described this particular house: "A three room well built adobe house, forty feet by seventeen and one-half feet, bearing north and south."

John Slaughter told him that he had hired a Mormon gardener, who had married two women. The house was built in such a manner that he could keep both wives. If one of them lived in Mexico, the U.S. Courts were not able to prosecute him. Some say that this Mormon was Ammon M. Tenney.

Tenney was born in Lee County, Iowa in November, 1844, which would make him the right age. He was a member of the Church of Jesus Christ of Latter Day Saints, and a Tenney family was known to have lived on the ranch. This Tenney had three wives: he married Anna Sariah Eager in 1867, Eliza Ann Udall in 1872, and Hettie Millicent Adams in 1890. The first wife he left in Colonia Diaz, Sonora.

Millicent Tenney McKellar, Tenney's first child by his third wife, Hettie, wrote an account in 1965 of her life on the ranch as a child, and described many of the family, employees, and items that were there.

Several Mormon families lived on the ranch at different times. Was this family of Tenney the one who lived in the Mormon house? It certainly seems so. Or was the story a joke fabricated by John Slaughter?

By the turn of the century there were a number of young people living on the San Bernardino. John and Viola wanted them to have as much education as possible. Towns that could provide such education, like Bisbee and Tombstone, were too far away to send the youngsters each day. They made a request to the Cochise County Board of Supervisors that they be allowed a school on the ranch. The Board understood the need and approved the establishment of a new school district at San Bernardino on October 8, 1902. It was labeled the Slaughter School District, Class 1, which meant that it had more than ten full time students, but less than twenty. This school began in the adobe house that John and Viola had lived in when they moved to the ranch in 1892.

Thomas Rynning, the second captain on the Arizona Rangers, made the desks and seats for the school children, living at the ranch while he did.

A Miss Glasgow, from Nebraska, was the first teacher at the school. Rosalie Newenham, from Illinois, was the second one. (She married Willie Slaughter.) The third teacher was Minnie Minus. (She married Willie Fitzgerald, a cowhand for the Chiricahua Cattle Company.)

During 1909-1910, sixteen pupils attended the school, their ages ranged from six to twenty years. Three of these pupils were wards of the Slaughters and the rest were children of the ranch employees. Eleven of them were from Mexico and two from the United States. This school district was suspended in 1924, then reinstated in 1928. It was closed forever on June 30, 1934.

Willie Slaughter was never very healthy. It seemed that he had inherited his father's lung problems.

He went to school in Tombstone, then in San Mateo, California at the St. Matthew's Academy. He also went to General City Business College in Quincy, Illinois.

In 1908, he went into the hardware business in Douglas. His health just did not allow him to be involved in work concerning the ranch.

Rosalie Newenham came to the San Bernardino to teach school. Willie married her in 1908.

After the marriage Willie's health grew worse. their son, William John, was born in 1909, and the couple moved to Phoenix in the hopes that the climate would help Willie. It was a vain hope and while there, their infant son died of meningitis.

In August, 1910, they moved back to Douglas. Their second son, John Horton Slaughter II, was born December 16, 1910. Willie died on August 23, 1911 of pulmonary tuberculosis. His funeral was held at the Douglas Masonic Hall. The funeral cortege had an honor escort of six mounted cowboys who rode by the hearse to the Cavalry Cemetery.

The ranch cemetery is located about one mile east and north of the ranch house. It looks toward Niggerhead Mountain. Today there are no identifying markers on the graves, but at least twenty-six bodies are buried there. A majority of the burials were those of the Mexican employees and their families. A ranch foreman named, Whisler, from Texas, was the first person buried in the little cemetery. Jake Bowman, killed by the Apaches in 1893, was the second. John Slaughter pulled out door and window casings from his ranch house to make a coffin for him.

The badmen buried there were put to their eternal rest by John Slaughter. Two of them, one named Childers, and one unknown, ambushed John on the ranch, jumping out of bushes and brandishing guns. John shot and killed both of them.

Another bad man killed by John and buried there was Arthur "Pegleg" Finney. Finney was a tin horn gambler, who also ran a shoeshine stand in Bisbee. For some reason he stole a horse in Naco and headed east for El Paso. Crossing the San Bernardino, he was tired out from all his activities, so he found a nice shade tree to take a nap under.

What Finney didn't know was that John Slaughter had seen him pass the house, although Finney had kept as far away as he could. John had called the American Customs House to inquire about him. The personnel there informed John that Finney was a thief and a wanted man. Judge Starr Williams of Bisbee ordered John to arrest Finney. He cautioned John that he was a bad man and would likely put up a fight; in the event that he did, John was to take him dead or alive.

When he went to make the arrest John took a ranch hand named Rios, Lloyd Gilman, W.J. Chillis and Jimmy Howell with him. They found Finney about a mile away, asleep under a tree.

What they did not know was that Finney had put his pistol in his right hand with his forefinger on the trigger and his thumb on the hammer. He had then rolled to his right side facing downward.

John walked up to Finney, picked up his rifle and threw it several feet away. It was the only weapon in sight. When Slaughter told him he was under arrest, he rolled over and came up with a cocked pistol in his hand, pointed straight at John. Without any hesitation John shot him with his .45.85 caliber Marlin rifle.

John's bullet struck Finney in the right hand, passing all the way through and into the right side of the breast. He had instructed Rios and Gilman to shoot when he did. They followed those instructions and both shot Finney. He was shot through the heart, the head, and the hip.

An excerpt from the coroner's jury read:

> "That he was a native of Texas, aged about 28 years, that he came to his death on the 19th day of September, A.D. 1898, in said county and territory....from the effects of three gunshot wounds while resisting arrest. Inflicted by Deputy U.S. Marshall John H. Slaughter and his assistants, Lloyd Gilman, and one Rios, while in charge of his official duties as such officer, and we hereby unanimously exonerate the said officer and party of all criminal proceedings. All of which we fully certify to by this verdict, in writing, by us signed this 20th day of September, A.D. 1898."

Ed A. Wittig	H.B. Strauss
David Johnson	Art Markeim
Peter Hanson	Charles L. Jones

The official coroner's certificate of death read: "I caused to be interred his body on the 20th day of September, A.D. 1898 at San Bernardino Ranch in said county and territory."

Arthur Finney was buried in the ranch cemetery with little ceremony and now lies there forgotten except by a few historians.

John Slaughter did say that when he looked down the barrel of Finney's pistol, it looked twice its actual size.

Cowboys, who were full time employees slept in the bunkhouse. At times extra hands had to be hired and these slept in the big hay barn tack room with the Mexican cowhands. These part time employees were usually Yaqui Indians. They were excellent riders and ropers. Although it seems an unfair practice the Mexican and Yaqui hands were paid ten dollars a month while the Anglos were paid thirty-five.

The ranch payroll varied with the number of cowhands employed while the number of employees were determined by the number of cattle that were on the ranch. Customarily, ranchers hired a foreman and two hands for a thousand head of cattle, and a foreman and five hands for five thousand head.

Slaughter had several thousand head of cattle. When an annual roundup was held there would be forty or fifty cowboys working it. Ranch owners from Arizona, New Mexico, and old Mexico would be there cutting their stock out of the huge herd, branding them and driving them away.

Employees who had families, lived in shacks all over the ranch on both sides of the international border. Because so many people lived on the ranch and because it was a long distance to any town, (Bisbee, 45 miles, and Tombstone, 65 miles), the Slaughters operated a small store, handling such staples as rice, flour, beans, coffee, cotton material, and hard candy. Some of the residents took their wages in supplies from the store.

In the late 1890's, Slaughter drilled into the artesian wells, and at a depth of 550 feet, he discovered a vast, underground supply of water. This seemingly inexhaustible source of water made his ranch a much more valuable piece of property. John created a one acre lake by erecting a rock and concrete dam to retain water from several springs. The lake soon contained ducks, fish, and Louisiana bullfrogs. From his underground water he piped ten wells to the surface for his cattle and ranch house.

Slaughter also began piping water to begin farming. The marsh land was drained and over 500 acres were put into cultivation in wheat, barley, beans, and cotton.

This attracted many Chinese to the area and a number of them became ranch employees. Large settlements of Chinese were in Sinaloa and Sonora because it was easy for immigrants to enter Mexico.

Most of the ranch Chinese lived together in a large adobe house on the Mexican side of the border where they raised crops on land watered by the San Bernardino springs. Three miles south of the border more Chinese lived at Chino Springs and farmed on the shares for Slaughter.

Some of the Chinese sold their produce in Bisbee and Douglas, driving wagon loads of fresh vegetables and ringing bells to let people know that they were coming.

One of these Chinese, named Lee, raised a garden on the shares with Slaughter. He would load his wagon and start for Douglas in the afternoon. It was about a three hour drive by wagon. The old man would camp overnight just outside Douglas and sleep until daylight. He would arrive in town very early with his load of fresh, crisp vegetables. Most of his produce was sold to the Phelps Dodge Mercantile Company, although other stores would buy what he had available.

As he had to leave Douglas before dark, Lee would arrive back at the ranch late at night because it was slow going in the dark. John always waited up for him. They would lay all the money that Lee had made on the table and count it. Then each of them would take his share.

Over the years the ranch had several Chinese cooks. John always preferred Negro cooks and firmly doubted the ability of any Chinese cook. Negroes did not like the isolation of the ranch and would not stay long. Finally, Viola persuaded him to hire a Chinese cook. Ah See worked on the ranch in 1900, Wi May Soo was there in 1910, and Lee On Loy arrived at a later date.

Normally Chinese are good cooks, and on the ranch they worked seven days a week, serving breakfast at 4:30 A.M. every morning. After lunch the cook would have a rest time before dinner.

Most Chinese kept their kitchen spotless and would not allow anyone else in it. Anyone who did use it, for any reason, had to leave it as clean as the Chinese cook had left it.

Many of the Chinese who lived on the Mexican side of the border did not have the necessary papers to enter the United States and would not cross the line. Mexico did not require them to have papers to live there.

In their dining room the Slaughter's standard of living was apparent; fine linen, silver, china, and only good manners were acceptable. Viola often remarked, "If a man owned a cow he ate in the family dining room. If he didn't he ate in the cowboy dining room." That was not totally correct as the cowboys were allowed to eat with the family--but few of them did. That was because Viola had too many rules for the table. Everyone there had to wear a coat and take off their spurs. Only Mr. Slaughter was allowed to wear his spurs to the table. Women could not wear divided riding skirts to that table. Any person who arrived after the meal had been completed, had to go into the kitchen, prepare their own food, then eat it in the cowboy dining room.

If the ranch had ten cowhands, plus the family, which consisted of fifteen, that meant that food had to be prepared to feed twenty-five people each meal. This did not include the large number of guests that appeared frequently.

Baking efforts alone required numerous piles of biscuits, pies, cookies, rolls, cornbread, and a minimum of thirty-five loaves of bread. Much of the food that was devoured was furnished by the ranch itself. Meat and milk came from the ranch cattle. Butter was brought from town in huge wooden tubs. Garden vegetables were grown in several locations. There was also a strawberry patch, a vineyard that yielded several kinds of grapes, and a number of orchard areas with apples, peaches, pears, figs, apricots, and other fruits.

When the icehouse was completed ice was hauled from Douglas by wagon, and unloaded by use of a chute. The cold storage could store three large steers. A huge refrigerator was also in this area for other foods, as was a large butcher block.

During the days of summer and fall the ranch people were busy canning and preserving fruit from the orchards, vegetables from the gardens, brandying grape preserves, and making wine. An impressive line of shelves, reaching from floor to ceiling, held the canned fruits, preserves and vegetables.

Jealous women envied Viola and her lifestyle: a lovely home, a good husband, a fine buggy, and a matched team of horses, (later the best of autos), a house boy, a cook, and a number of other servants. They were aware that Viola slept as long as she wished every morning and, that she bathed and dressed for dinner every day. In short, she had and did all the things that they yearned for, but were forbidden.

During their many years on the ranch Viola had a number of health problems. Among them were an ovarian pregnancy, a serious miscarriage, and numerous gall bladder problems, including surgery. At one point, everyone believed that she was dying, even her doctor. John went so far as to call a minister. Viola said it was the only time that she ever saw tears in the eyes of that tough old man. She struggled to survive and made an unbelievable recovery.

John Baptiste Hinnaut, a black man, could well have been Slaughter's most valuable employee. Everyone called him "Old Bat". Even he did not know how old he was. He had been born a slave, but had served in the Union Army during the War Between the States. Billy Slaughter had hired him in San Antonio to work on his ranch. When John brought his second herd to Arizona, he had borrowed Old Bat for the trip. Once they had arrived Old Bat just stayed. He enjoyed being the cook on trail drives and roundups, and the cowhands liked him because he was a good one. Soon he became John's bodyguard, because he knew that his boss carried a money belt full of gold coins. Most all business was conducted in cash in those days, and hard cash was demanded on most every occasion.

This old black man was loyal and faithful to the Slaughters all his life, and John Slaughter was quite fond of Old Bat. He always accompanied Slaughter on all his cattle buying trips into Mexico. A great deal of the time Old Bat wore the money belt with gold coins as few would suspect him of carrying a fortune in gold.

Once Slaughter took John Roberts, Old Bat, and $12,000 in silver into Mexico to purchase a herd of cattle. Word of this large amount of money leaked out, and the three men were trapped in a small Mexican village by about forty banditos who were most eager to obtain ownership of the saddlebags full of silver coin. Unable to find a place of refuge, the three Americans slipped out of town under the cover of darkness.

A cowboy on a lathered, worn out horse, rode into the San Bernardino ranch yard and gave Viola the startling news that her husband and his men had been murdered by Mexican bandits. She immediately set out for Mexico in her buckboard to recover the bodies. On the road to Magdalena, she met a herd of cattle. John Roberts, Old Bat, and John Slaughter were driving them.

They explained to a happy but bewildered Viola that they had slipped out of that Mexican village, and knowing that they would be followed, took refuge in some big rocks. When the bandits found them, Slaughter emptied several of the banditos saddles from their place of concealment. At this turn of events, the survivors decided that they did not want that silver enough to try to take it again; whereupon, John and his men continued on his cattle buying trip.

Most ranchers were afraid to carry large amounts of cash into Mexico; however, cattle were uncommonly cheap there and John Slaughter feared nothing, except lightning. B.A. Packard, a ranching neighbor, wanted to go with John on one of his buying trips into Mexico to see how he handled that part of his business. John loaded several bags of 'dobe' dollars onto a pack mule, handed the lead rope to Old Bat and rode out.

When they reached the hacienda where they intended to buy the cattle, John found that the cattle were old steers and not the young ones that he had been promised. However, the owner insisted that he take the old steers and leave the silver that was on the mule.

While talking to the Mexican, Slaughter had seen several heavily armed men in the shadows of an adobe wall. He realized that they were just waiting for a signal from their boss. John slowly rode over to the man and before anyone knew what he was doing, whipped out his shotgun, cocked both hammers and put the business end under the man's chin. Everyone was absolutely still some even holding their breaths.

John told Packard and Old Bat to take the mule and silver and ride on down the road and that he would meet them in a little while. They did and he did. There was no pursuit.

In the mid 1880's Old Bat married a young woman from Tombstone, named Lavinia. She was a good cook so she took over that position on the ranch. But, she was rather young and spoiled, so she and Old Bat argued continually. Finally, he sent her back to Tombstone and got a divorce.

When Old Bat grew too old to work, John retired him and supplied him with all the soft drinks and candy he desired. He was quite healthy right up to the time he died at the ranch, on January 17, 1919. His funeral was held at the Negro church in Douglas and he was buried there.

Viola said this about Old Bat:

"He was very faithful and we feel as though we have lost a member of the family. I firmly believe that he was loved by more people than the majority of us are. He was as brave as his character was beautiful."

John Swain Slaughter, another black man, was born a slave on July 18, 1845. Although he did become an employee and friend of John Slaughter, he did not meet Slaughter until 1872, several years after he had been freed.

Slaughter needed domestic help and found John Swain and his mother in San Antonio, homeless and starving. He hired her and allowed her to keep the young boy with her. She was the cook on his Atascosa County ranch for several years. She became ill and died before Slaughter moved to Arizona. She left her son, John Swain, in his care.

Viola said,,"the colored man, John Swain, was my first house boy, not Mr. Slaughter's bodyguard." Some writers have confused John Swain and Old Bat.

John Swain became an expert tracker and an excellent shot. Once, he reported to Slaughter that a large herd of his cattle had been driven across the boundary into Mexico.

Slaughter, Old Bat, John Swain, and several Mexican cowboys trailed the cattle to a village deep in Sonora.

The cattle were being watched by herders who fled when they saw the Americans coming. John knew of the man who took the cattle because he was a well known bandit along the border. He was also the chief of a band of about a dozen unscrupulous bandits.

John and his men started the herd of cattle back toward the San Bernardino with Slaughter riding rear guard. When he saw the rustlers coming up behind them he turned the cattle into a canyon and took up a defensive position. That was when Slaughter realized that the total number of defenders were only three. The Mexicans had deserted him. He and the two loyal black men were armed with double barreled shotguns. When the bandits rushed them, these shotguns began to roar and take a heavy toll on the bandits. They turned tail, rode away, and did not come back.

When the Slaughters moved to the San Bernardino ranch, John Swain did not go with them. He stayed in Tombstone, married, and worked around the mines until the boom was over. Following that he was employed as the janitor at the Cochise County Courthouse until 1931. During his last years he lived in a small house on the outskirts of Tombstone. He died on February 8, 1945, in the Douglas hospital....he was almost 100 years old.

John Swain was laid to rest in Tombstone's Boothill with military honors, including a final rifle salute. His tombstone reads:

JOHN SWAIN SLAUGHTER

Born June 1845. Former Slave who came to Tombstone 1879. Died February 8, 1945. Erected by the personnel at Fort Huachuca and Friends of Tombstone In Memory of a Worthy Pioneer

CEMETERY OCCUPANTS

Dolores Ramirez was a Yaqui Indian who worked and lived on the ranch for many years. His widow named those she remembered:

Loreto Ramirez (baby)
Francisco Valacas (child)
Rosalia Ramirez (baby)
Josepha Valacas (child)
Ignacio Cupis
Ramon Mejia
Marcelo Mejia
Jose Matuz
Jose Escalante
Manuel Cupis
    Thomas (child)
    Thomas (child)
    Thomas (child)
Juana Soto
Juana Alvarez
Ramona Molispa
Francisco Estrella
    Vamuea (child)
    Vamuea (child)
    Vamuea (child)
Fernando Enriquez
    Whisler
    Childers
Ygnacio
Jake Bowman
Gabriel
Vasquez (child)
Apache May
Arthur Finney
Lorenza Molina (baby)
Jesus Wilson

RANCH EMPLOYEES

Frank Anderson
George Baker
Wake Benge
Billy Claibourne
Jesus Cesaro
Thomas Cochran
Joe Feidley
Felegardo Felez
Francisco Felez
Arthur Fisher Sr.
Jesse Fisher
Pedro Garcia
Luperto Gomez
Billy Grounds
Will Hicks
Will Hildreth
James Howell
Stonewall Howell
Thomas Howell
Charles Jones
Louis Jorgenson
Loreto Laborin
Jeff Lewis
Wi May Soo

Jesus Mendez
Clarence Minus
Antonio Molino
Miguel Moreno
?? Mortenson
James Potter
William Potter
Jose Renleri
John Roberts
N.H. Robinson
Danyan Robles
Tad Rowland
Valentin Sedano
Al Shropshire
Simon Soria
John Stith
Hugh Taylor
A.M. Tenner
William Watkins
Whisler
Steele Woods
John Hinnaut
Ah See
Lee On Loy

— Longhorn steers on the San Bernardino —

— Cowboy bunkhouse —

— Addie Slaughter —

— 1884 - First house built on the ranch —
Destroyed by an earthquake

— Willie Slaughter —
John's only son

— Slaughter school district, 1903 —

— Minnie Minus Slaughter —
with niece May Watkins and John Slaughter - 1902

— John Slaughter, Hugh Conlin & B.A. Packard —
Cattlemen

Slaughter ranch school house

— The San Bernardino barn —

— May - the chinese cook —

— John and Viola —
eating watermelon with friends

— Mary Ann (Grandma) Howell —

— Old Bat and Viola —

— The San Bernardino store —

— Howell family plot —
*Tombstone City Cemetery.
Stonewall, Amazon and Mary Ann are buried here.*

John Horton Slaughter *(l)* & Charles Holmes Slaughter *(r)*

— John Slaughter's ranch house —

— John Slaughter, family and employees —

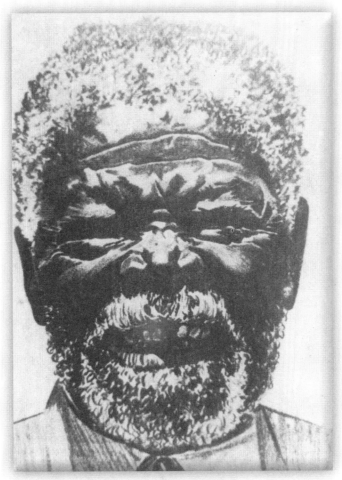

— Old Bat —
John Baptiste Hinnaut

— John Swain Slaughter —
came to Tombstone with John Slaughter

— Slaughter ranch cemetery - 1990 —

— **Death Certificate - Stonewall J. Howell** —
Died of pneumonia on October 22, 1889

— **Death Certificate - John Baptiste Hinnaut** —
Died of intestinal obstruction on January 17, 1919

Sources:

Tombstone Prospector, May 3, 1887

Southwest Stockman, Willcox, September 26, 1889

Tombstone Epitaph, April 28, 1893

Tombstone Prospector, February 3, 1897

District Court, First Judicial District, County of Cochise, Territory of Arizona, Inquest held on the body of Arthur Finney (alias PegLeg) September 28, 1898

Tombstone Prospector, March 16, 1903

Douglas Daily Dispatch, September 9, 1903

Bisbee Daily Review, January 25, 1906

Ibid August 25, 1911

Earthquake History of the United States,

N.H. Heck, 1928

Bisbee Daily Review, February 28, 1941

⁓APACHE MAY⁓

Although Geronimo and his "hostiles" had surrendered in 1886 and had been deported to Florida, some of the "broncos" had not surrendered and were still raiding in Arizona ten years later in 1896.

So, ten years after Geronimo had departed Arizona, a few Apaches "jumped" the San Carlos Reservation. They had tired of the monotonous life that denied them the thrill of raiding and killing. Early on that year the Apaches attacked the Merril ranch near Ash Springs on the Gila River, slaughtering Horatio Merrill and his young daughter, Eliza. This young girl had a white dress, or basque, tight at the waist, shaped by darts and many buttons down the front. The Apaches carried away many of the Merrill's possessions, among them this white dress and a fringed, brown, woolen shawl.

Alfred Hand, a remote rancher on Cave Creek in the San Simon Valley, was also brutally murdered by these same raiders. Among the items they took from his cabin was a Cochise County election poster made of white muslin, listing the names of the Republican candidates in the election of 1888. Strangely enough, included in this list was the name of Si H. Bryant, who had been defeated by John Slaughter that election.

Slaughter had long been losing cattle to Apaches on the Mexican portion of his ranch. When his foreman, Jesse Fisher, reported that he had located a "bronco" camp in the mountains, John sent a message to army troops that he knew were camped a few miles away in Guadalupe Canyon.

The unit commander was Second Lieutenant N.K. Averill, and he received Slaughter's message at 8:30 P.M. on May 5,

That Wicked Little Gringo

1896. Averill assembled his men and rode to Slaughter's ranch, arriving a few minutes past midnight.

Because he knew that he would be going into Mexico illegally, Averill was anxious to get started before anyone could order him not to go. But John Slaughter would not be hurried. They finally departed the ranch just before sunrise on May 6, 1896.

When they rode into Mexico and reached the Guadalupe Mountains they were met by Jesse Fisher and another Slaughter hired hand. These two men raised the party total to seventeen men.

Fisher guided them to the Apache camp that he had found, but it was deserted. The Apache scouts said that its occupants had abandoned it several days ago. From appearances it probably was a permanent camp for the Apaches.

The Camp was located on the highest peak in the area and was enclosed on three sides by sheer rock walls. Only one very narrow trail led into the camp. The Apaches had used rocks to build fortifications and then disguised them to appear as natural formations. Though the camp was deserted, it seemed to have been occupied for a long tine. The scouts read all the signs then said that the camp had been used by four men, seven women, two children, and ten horses. They also said that the Apaches had left the camp because of an insufficient water supply.

The Apache scouts unraveled the broncos' trail and led the pursuers to the new hostile camp which was about twenty miles away. In order to surprise the Apaches, two men and the horses were left behind at midnight and the men moved on to the camp on foot. The Apaches had camped on a hill where four deep canyons came together, so it was impossible to completely surround them. Averill and Slaughter moved their men into position about daybreak.

The hostiles must have seen or heard them, as they began shooting at them. Both sides fired several times with no positive results. Averill and Slaughter had the Apaches outgunned so the Indians just melted into rough country country so wild that the white men could not follow.

When the Apaches left the camp the white men found supplies of dried meat, corn, acorns, mesquite beans, sugar, salt, and skin bags filled with water. These items were packed in such a manner that indicated that the Apaches were getting ready to leave.

Seven saddles and bridles were also found in the camp, plus a great deal of plunder stolen from the Americans and Mexicans: hatchets, knives, scissors, needles, thread, horseshoeing tools, reloading equipment, black powder and lead, rugs, blankets, pieces of leather, and $1.25 in U.S. coins. Some Indian ponies and nine head of stolen horses were also in the camp, four of the latter belonging to the Slaughters. One of the four was Viola's mare, Dixie.

John Slaughter went into one of the wickiups and in a pile of cloth and blankets he found a small Apache girl that was about one year old. He wrapped her into a brown, woolen shawl lying nearby and took her back to his ranch.

Once back at the San Bernardino it was discovered that the child's shirt waist had been cut down from a larger garment.....which was identified as being made from the clothing of the murdered Eliza Merrill. The brown woolen shawl that Slaughter had wrapped around the little waif had also belonged to Eliza. The child's dress was made from a curious item-- Cochise County election poster, the one stolen from Alfred Hand's cabin after the Apaches killed him.

The Slaughters named the child Apache May for the month in which they had found her. Another foster child on the ranch, Lola Robles called her "Pache", which quickly became "Patchy".

Viola dressed her in beautiful bright colors and kept her neat and clean. All the people on the ranch helped take good care of her. Everyone in southeast Arizona was curious about the little Apache. When it became known that she had been dressed in clothing taken from those murdered by her band of Apaches, many remarked, "You can never tame an Apache!"

Viola and John took Patchy to Tombstone in order that curious people might see her. As well, they wanted C.S. Fly, a close friend of John's and a photographer, to take some pictures of her.

The Tombstone Epitaph, June 17, 1896, read:

"Mrs. J.H. Slaughter and charming daughter, Miss Addie arrived in town today with the little Apache papoose from the San Bernardino ranch."

"As soon as it became known that the papoose was in town, a steady stream of people visited Fly's Gallery to catch a glimpse of the young captive.

"Isn't she cute, said each of the ladies in their turn as the youngster sat mutely but calmly, munching on some cake. When our office devil arrived, his face and hands besmirched with ink and his new shirt dobbed in spots, the papoose immediately cast a smile of recognition. Her features were covered with a most propitious smile and she seemed tickled to death, which in turn, was contagious to the ladies present."

"The papoose is a chubby girl of about two or three years of age, with a good head of coarse, black hair, large beautiful eyes, and for her size, is strong and healthy, and a complexion that color which distinguishes an Apache. The little papoose in her neat, red dress, clean face and parted hair makes her look indeed 'cute!'"

"Mrs. Slaughter, who has inquired into the matter, and finding its mother has not returned to the reservation, has decided to adopt and raise the papoose. The entire family has become quite attached to the young captive, and if she takes kindly to civilized life will no doubt receive a liberal education, and be brought up in the way it should go. Mrs. Slaughter states 'Apache', as she has already been christened, takes kindly to her surroundings, and has become the pet of the San Bernardino ranch."

In the fall of 1896, little Arthur Fisher came to live on the ranch. The two girls, Apache May and Lola liked little Arthur immensely and the children became a threesome. All of them were well liked by all the adults that came into contact with them.

Slaughter frequently did business with the Gabilondo brothers, who lived in Mexico about forty miles south of the border. They ran cattle on their Guadalupe Canyon Ranch, the 3G brand in Sonora, just outside Cuchuverachi. The brothers made little chairs, by hand for the three children, then rode north on horseback to deliver them in person.

It was quite obvious that though Patchy liked all the people on the ranch, John Slaughter was the favorite person in her world. Apparently, he felt the same way about her. She called him Don Juan and followed him about the ranch whenever she could. When he left the ranch, she would sit for hours waiting for him to return. Her happiest moments were when she was allowed to ride a horse with Don Juan.

There were times when her Indian heritage appeared and she became sullen, silent, and stubborn. It was then that she was all Apache. Once, when Viola sternly reprimanded her, Patchy resented it and screamed, "When I grow up, I will kill you!"

One cold morning in February 1900, the children were playing around a fire that had been built out in the yard. They were poking sticks into the flames when Patchy's clothes caught on fire. The sight of her burning clothing terrified her and she fled running away from the house. She ran so fast that it took Willie Slaughter some time to catch her and smother the flames. By the time that this had been done, a good part of her body had been severely burned.

Today, Douglas is about eighteen miles from the Slaughter ranch, but in early 1900 Douglas was not there. In those days the nearest doctor was in Bisbee, forty five miles away. There was a telephone line to Bisbee and Dr. Dudley was called and

That Wicked Little Gringo

appraised of the situation. The doctor gave instructions over the phone and started for the ranch at once. But it would be more that eight hours before he would complete that forty-five miles, driving a team.

Patchy told John Slaughter, "Don Juan, I'm going to die." She suffered all day and when Dr. Dudley arrived he found the little Apache in shock and her vitality extremely low. He informed the Slaughters that he had no hope at all for her recovery. Apache May died the next morning.

Jesse Fisher made a tiny coffin of rough lumber and lined and covered it with cloth. Patchy was laid to her final rest in the ranch cemetery.

Apache Slaughter — "Patchy"
with election poster dress and Eliza Merrill's shawl and under waist

C.S. Fly Photo

Apache May
Indian girl adopted by the Slaughters

Ruth Shaw and Viola holding Apache May's wardrobe

Apache May playing outsie the Slaughter home

Ruth Shaw at Apache May's grave
in the Slaughter ranch cemetery.

Sources:

Solomon Bulletin, December 6, 1895
National Archives, Washington, D.C. (military)
Tombstone Prospector, May 12, 1896
Tombstone Epitaph, June 3, 1896
Tombstone Epitaph, June 17, 1896
Douglas Daily Dispatch, October 3, 1926

REVOLUTION!

During the stormy years of revolution in Mexico which occurred during 1910-1929, all the border towns and ranches were affected. A military outpost was maintained at the San Bernardino during many of those years.

A permanent post never materialized at the ranch. The force there consisted of a number of tents, set up on the mesa, across the lake from the Slaughter ranch house. The entire purpose of this outpost was simply to protect American life and property. Nogales, Naco, and Douglas were all of vast importance to the Mexican Insurrectos as it was necessary that they have a place where they could gain recruits, contraband, and refuge, should a Federal force be too strong. Federalists did not want the Insurrectos to have such an advantage. In order to prevent it, they had to control the border towns. Battles were fought for this control in 1911, 1913, 1914, and 1915.

Following the battle at Agua Prieta (across the border from Douglas) in 1915, there was no more fighting in that area. However, American leaders feared that the country might be invaded by Germany or by some of the various and sundry armies in Mexico.

Most of the violent activity for some time was mainly in the Mexican states of Sonora and Chihuahua. The Insurrectos were not well organized and their desertions to other rebel armies or even to the Federalist army were not unusual. The majority of Americans, who lived in the border area, seemed to sympathize with the Insurrectos rather than with the government troops.

That Wicked Little Gringo

John Slaughter was a rancher with a very large ranch, much of it in Mexico. As a man, who bought and sold cattle in both Sonora and Arizona, he was in a very precarious position. He and Viola were on friendly terms with a number of Mexican officials as well as some of the best families in Mexico.

One of John's friends below the border was Colonel Emilio Kosterlitzky, the head of the tough Rurales. They had been friends since the days when John had lived in Charleston. Emilio still cooperated with the Arizona Rangers in removing criminals from society on both sides of the border.

Kosterlitzky was born in Russia on November 16, 1853. During the early 1870's while serving in the Russian Imperial Navy, he jumped ship in Venezuela. In April, 1873, he enlisted in the Mexican cavalry at Guaymas. Emilio became an excellent soldier and somehow also became a favorite of Porfirio Diaz, who ruled Mexico for thirty-five years.

He was involved in the Yaqui, Maya, and Apache wars, fighting with loyalty and bravery. But he is best remembered as the leader of the Rurales, the toughest, most merciless horsemen on the continent. His troops were recruited from Mexican jails and prisons. Criminals did have a choice -- they could join his Cordada or face a firing squad. Rurales obeyed all orders promptly. It they did not, death was the penalty. Regardless of his tactics, he did bring law and order to Mexico.

He was handsome, intelligent, and attentive, and Viola said that she liked him, but that he told monstrous lies. She could not understand why he told such horrible, bloody, tales of the cruel things that he had done. Authors note: (Viola did not know that the tales he told were true and he was not lying. Wherever his Rurales rode they left a bloody trail behind them. She saw him only as a guest at the ranch ... not riding as the jefe of the Rurales). His Rurales killed hundreds of people in Mexico and there is no doubt but what many of them needed killing.

Kosterlitzky served the Gendarmeria Fiscal from 1885 until 1913. When the revolutionists were coming into power, he knew that he was finished. Legend says that General Pedro Ojeda and he fought their way through a mob in Naco to obtain asylum from U.S. authorities, and that Kosterlitzky surrendered a sword still wet with blood to the American commander, Cornelius C. Smith.

The truth is that Kosterlitzky surrendered himself and his men to Captain Smith involving none of the legend. It was done quietly and without fanfare in Nogales.

Emilio went to work for the Department of Justice in Los Angeles. His knowledge of Mexico plus his ability to speak German, French, English, Danish, Swedish, Polish, Italian, Russian, and Spanish, made him a most valued agent. He was never in Mexico again.

Both Federal and Rebel troops found the Mormon settlements too tempting to ignore. Colonia Morales and Colonia Oaxaca were attacked and brutally ravaged several times. All over Sonora in 1912 the rebels also attacked many of the mines... Cananea, Nacozari, and El Tigre. Many of the miners were killed. The miners and the Saints fought back to protect their families, homes, property, and jobs.

Slaughter helped them the best he could because they were his friends. He bought weapons and ammunition, packaged it, and shipped it to Colonia Morales in wagons driven by young boys.

Conditions grew even worse in Sonora. Mines cut back drastically on all their operations, and by late in 1912, a large number of the Saints had departed Sonora and returned to the United States. In April 1913, Joseph Smith gave official permission to abandon the Mormon colonies in Mexico.

Late in October, 1915, Pancho Villa and his army, numbering approximately 10,000 men, arrived and set up camp on the Mexican side of Slaughter's ranch. These men had come from Casas Grandes across the Sierra Madres and were tired, thirsty and starving. They had had no beans, flour, or meat, and very little water during the past two days. It did not take them long to devour Slaughter's cornfields and fifty head of his cattle without consulting him.

John stood on the front porch of his house and watched his beef and corn disappear down the throats of Villa's soldiers. Muttering to himself for a while John finally told a cowhand to bring his shotgun and his horse. When Viola asked where he was going and what he intended doing, he answered, "I say, I say, I'm gonna ride down and jump old Pancho Villa!"

Holding the shotgun over his saddle horn, the seventy-four year old Slaughter rode right through Villa's army, and up to the general himself. He and Pancho knew one another as Villa had been a guest at the ranch a number of times. John had a serious talk with old Pancho and when he returned to the ranch it was with his saddlebags full of nice, shiny, twenty dollar gold pieces. Villa had paid him for his cattle.

When Villa lined his army out for Agua Prieta, the cannons on wheels, wagons, and horse soldiers reached from just outside Douglas back to the Slaughter ranch. Because of this impending battle, American military strength in Douglas had been increased to 6,500 troops. More of these were sent to strengthen the Slaughter ranch outpost.

Pancho Villa was soundly defeated in the battle at Agua Prieta in November, 1915. Instrumental in his loss was that, unknown to Villa at the time, General Calles' Federal troops had been reinforced by rail through United States property. In addition, Calles had three very powerful searchlights plus mines which the defenders could explode electrically. Cross firing machine guns protected trenches, and a maze of barbed wire entanglements were included in their defense.

The battle lasted eighteen hours until Villa withdrew to the west, leaving the battlefield cluttered with his dead and wounded. Villa's downfall had actually begun at Celaya, where the battle was fought in 1915, on April 6th, 7th, 13th, and 15th. Obregon had increased his army to a total of 22,000 men. Villa's army numbered only 15,000 fighting men, but he believed that his cavalry was superior to that of Obregon and would ride right over them. The bloody fight that ensued was a disaster for Villa — thousands of his men were killed. He lost 12,000 men because Obregon ordered all wounded and prisoners executed.

Following this defeat, part of Villa's army arrived at the Slaughter ranch tired, hungry, and thirsty. They were begging for food, but Viola contacted the mesa outpost and asked if she could feed them. She was given permission to do so and she fed a large number of the pathetic soldiers, many of them just boys.

A Villa officer came to the ranch house unarmed. Any traveler or visitor was always welcomed at the ranch and hospitality was extended. The officer was invited into the house, fed a good meal, and given a comfortable bed for the night.

He had a large amount of money and wanted to pay the Slaughters for their generosity to him and his soldiers. Of course, the Slaughters refused payment. It was the code of the west.

When the merciless battles were fought for control of Agua Prieta in 1911 and 1915, the citizens of Douglas were continually exposed to gunfire and artillery shells. In the 1911 battle, two civilians were killed, and in the 1915 battle, one civilian and one Army private, Harry. J. Jones, were killed. Several other civilians were wounded. (The military camp at Douglas was named Camp Harry J. Jones in the private's honor. It was approved on February 28, 1916.)

Americans went absolutely insane during these battles. They would gather in large groups and cheer the Rebels even when the bullets splattered all around them. During any sort of lull in the fighting, sight-seers would dash across the border and onto the battlefield to gather souvenirs and take photographs.

When the battle at Naco took place all the hotels and other available rooms were filled the entire time. Spectators arrived in Naco, Arizona by the train load and the road from Bisbee to Naco was jammed with traffic.

That Wicked Little Gringo

As the 1915 battle for Agua Prieta began, school officials of Douglas and Pirtleville closed all the public schools because of safety concerns. The "Villa Vacation" extended from Monday through Thursday. The only thing this accomplished was that it increased the number of spectators in the danger area, as all of the teachers and students, freed from school, went down to watch the battle.

In view of some of the ridiculous actions by the populace, the Douglas Daily Dispatch printed "A Rule to Observe When Picnics Are Held in Front of Battles". The advice followed: "Do not run to the skirmish line and peer down the muzzle of a rifle!"

This insane excitement even overwhelmed Viola. She had some friends who were going to Agua Prieta so she put her saddle on the fender of their car and went along with them. John had been away on a cattle buying trip, but arrived in Douglas just in time to intercept Viola. She complained that she did not get to see any of the bodies and gore.

There were numerous acts of kindness during this insanity. Douglas citizens spent a great deal of time finding containers, filling them with water, and carrying them over the border to the thirsty Mexican soldiers. The seriously wounded men on both sides were cared for in American hospitals. Douglas also provided a camp for the endless stream of refugees coming across the border.

Pancho Villa grew very angry at the United States when he discovered that they had assisted General Calles in his defeat at Agua Prieta. In a rage, he threatened to turn his artillery on Douglas.

As a reprisal Villa stopped a train at Santa Isabel, Chihuahua in January, 1916, and murdered fifteen American engineers that were aboard.

Villa attacked the tiny town of Columbus, New Mexico on the night of March 9, 1916. It seems that he was making an attempt to start a war between the United States and Mexico. His raiders killed seventeen people, nine of which were civilians...one of those was a woman.

General "Black Jack" Pershing and the U.S. Army chased Villa all over Mexico during most of 1916 and part of 1917. They could never catch the wily Villa because he was in his own back yard. When the army was pulled out of Mexico, Pancho Villa became a Mexican folk hero. The government retired him in 1920 as a general. Villa was assassinated in Parral in 1923. In 1926, grave robbers stole his head. Villa's skull has never been recovered.

Villa's attack on Columbus caused the army to increase their manpower at Slaughter's ranch by two companies. During the years of the Mexican revolution the outpost was used as a base for patrolling the International Border. Patrols of ten men each were sent out east, to the Animas Valley in New Mexico. When it was rumored that Villa was going to return and attack Agua Prieta the outpost force was increased to 600 men, both infantry and cavalry units.

John Slaughter had little use for the army or its people until he found that they would play poker with him. After that, he and the outpost soldiers became great friends, because John would rather gamble than do anything. He was anxious for a game every night.

Outpost duty was usually very boring, but one day in January, 1918, there was unexpected action for a while. Captain David H. Blakelock and Second Lieutenant George J. Lind were out hunting rabbits a few yards north of the border when they were suddenly surrounded by Mexicans.

They were disarmed and taken to an adobe building located about a mile below the border. When the situation became known in camp, several soldiers, against standing orders, went over the border and rescued the two officers. In the course of this rescue, they shot and killed two Mexicans. This created an international incident which the two countries argued over for years.

After 1918, the San Bernardino outpost was used for rifle practice and training marches and little else. Camp Harry J. Jones was closed in 1933 and the outpost was abandoned altogether at the same time.

John Horton Slaughter

John Slaughter's home and 1-1/4 acre pond

— Slaughter ranch outpost —

THE OUT TRAIL

In 1906, the Democratic Party of Cochise County badgered John Slaughter into entering the political field by pressuring him to run for the 24th Territorial Assembly.

Although his heart really wasn't in such a move, he agreed. In spite of his attitude, John led the county ticket in his election as assemblyman. His majority was more than 1,000 and in those days that was a bunch. As was his custom, John remained a man of few words and let the other politicians make the flowery speeches and introduce the bills.

One of his main endeavors was to establish a territorial penitentiary branch at Benson, Arizona. To him, Yuma was a poor location, and he knew the costs involved in the transporting of prisoners all the way across the territory from his days as county sheriff.

He did accept the chairmanship of the assembly's County Boundaries, Agricultural and Public Buildings Committees. John did not care much for politics or the people involved in them, and he certainly did not relish living in the Adams Hotel in Phoenix. Viola, too, did not like the politician's methods of conducting business and she liked their wives even less. When his term was over they were more than happy to go back to the ranch.

In October, 1900, several men met in Bisbee and decided to start a new town on the border. They were James Douglas, John Slaughter, C.D. Beckwith, S.W. Slawson, M.J. Cunningham, and S.W. French. Douglas was an expert in minerals and an employee of the Phelps Dodge Mining Company. He eventually became the company president. Douglas' efforts and the massive copper ore belt that ran across southeast Arizona and Sonora were the foundation on which the town was built. It was named Douglas in his honor.

These men organized the International Land and Improvement Company with James Douglas as its president. The company laid out a townsite and E.G. Howe made a map of it on January 12, 1901.

To build their city Slaughter and his associates brought into existence the Douglas Improvement Company. They envisioned a modern town, with very wide streets, electricity, a telephone system, an ice plant, and an adequate water supply system. And that is what they built.

John and Viola went to the St. Louis World's Fair Exposition in 1904. They took Old Bat with them for the purpose of taking him to Hot Springs, Arkansas, to take the hot mineral baths for his rheumatism.

Slaughter was apparently fond of the meat business, as he bought a butcher shop in Bisbee for $2,500 from J.E. Mosher in February, 1910. A short time later, he purchased another butcher business from F.W. Arndt for $650.51.

Charley Clawson and John Slaughter owned a large part of the land around Douglas. They were among the organizers of the Bank of Douglas. Slaughter built the San Bernardino Building on Nineteenth Street. By 1912, the rent on this building was $75 a month. John spent a lot of time in Douglas conducting business and playing poker in the Gadsden Hotel. Jim East, an old friend, was Douglas Chief of Police.

Buying his first automobile in 1912, John had a sudden desire to see old Texas friends and the places of his beginnings...Friotown and Pleasanton. Now that he had an automobile he rode back to Texas in style, in the back seat with a chauffeur. He made two such trips, one in 1914, and one in 1920. John visited with the old timers who were still alive. They told tales of the past that they all remembered, and drove about the countryside, which was still much as he remembered.

John, Viola, Edith Stowe, and other friends attended the World's Fair in San Francisco in 1915, then went down the coast to visit in Long Beach and San Diego.

As did most of the old time cattlemen, John liked good whiskey. Still if good whiskey was not to be had, they would drink whatever was available. Prohibition bothered the Slaughters not at all. Old Bat helped John bury barrels and jugs of whiskey and mescal about the ranch. Although it was illegal, visitors were treated to a few drinks of this liquid treasure. Even the Rurales stopped by for a drink when they were in the vicinity.

Jesse Fisher, a cousin to Viola, had come to Tombstone in the early 1880's just for a visit, but decided to stay. He became a close friend of John Slaughter's and eventually the foreman on the San Bernardino Ranch. Jesse was 200 pounds, six feet, blonde haired, and well known for his truthfulness. He was not foreman long until he began to carry a money belt filled with $10,000 in gold coins. This was necessary as he bought and sold cattle for the ranch. Old Bat was a bodyguard for Jesse just as he had been for John in bygone years. John had chosen the right man this time. Jesse was allowed to run his own cattle herd on the ranch, branded with his own Lazy B.

During the years 1889-1890 Fisher was Sheriff Slaughter's jailer and special deputy. He knew the country well, and at times, went along with Slaughter when he raided the Apaches, scouted for the Army, or chased outlaws.

Jesse did have a difficult time refusing anyone. Sometimes, he even signed notes for his friends when he knew the notes were worthless. Viola said that Jesse once made considerable money on his beef herd and that he took these profits and opened a meat market in Douglas. Then because he was involved with the ranch, he had his brother manage his meat market. His brother managed it so much that Jesse went bankrupt.

Fisher always maintained that he was born to be a bachelor. But, that was before Mary (Mame) Graham came from Columbus, Ohio to live with her sister, Mrs. George Kelsey. Within just a few months, Jesse decided that perhaps bachelor life really wasn't all that shiny. Jesse and Mame were married in the parsonage of the Church of the Immaculate Conception in Douglas on October 24, 1907.

Jesse soon left the employment of the Slaughters and opened a one room meat market on Tenth Street in Douglas. He did well selling beef to the El Paso and Southwestern Railroad. He acquired a small ranch on the outskirts of town and built a large slaughter house to supply his meat market. In town, he built a house with eleven rooms for his family. He and Mame had two boys, Edward and Gerald.

In the spring of 1921, John Slaughter called Jesse and asked him to do just one more roundup for him. Fisher did not really want to do it, but he knew that old John was eighty years old and unable to do much work anymore. He just could not refuse the old man who had been such a good friend for so long.

Slaughter still kept gold in his ranch safe just as he had always done. Afterward, everyone involved remarked that things were just too calm on that night of May 4, 1921. Jesse had decided to stay late at the ranch that night and had called his wife in Douglas to inform her of his intentions.

Viola noticed that it was growing late and that Manuel, the chore boy about the ranch, had not appeared for supper — nor had he fastened up the young turkeys and chickens. As none of the fowl would survive the night out in the open, Viola sent Jesse with Edith Stowe to ensure the security of the chicken coops, while she took care of the turkeys. All three of them left the house at the same time.

Evidently, Fisher heard someone in the commissary and called out to them. Later, Edith said that she and Jesse had finished closing the chickens in their coops and had started back to the house. When they passed the bunkhouse the door opened a crack. Frightened, Edith ran toward the house. Before she reached it she heard shots. When she looked back she saw Fisher fall. She did not see anyone, but Viola saw Manuel and Jose Perez rush out of the bunk house.

Running into the house, Viola screamed to John, "Manuel has killed Jesse!" John picked up his pistol and prepared to go outside and find the killers; however, the women were terrified, believing that the house was surrounded by bandits. Slaughter sat down, facing the front door, pistol in hand, waiting for whatever happened next.

Viola called their son-in-law, Dr. William Greene, then she called Percy Bowden, Douglas Chief of Police. Bowden in turn called the sheriff's office. Dr. Greene arrived at the ranch a short time after the lawmen. When he examined Fisher's body, he found three bullet wounds, two through the shoulder blade, and one through the stomach. The wounds indicated that two guns of different caliber had been used. Jesse had died instantly. Bloody footprints led toward the commissary.

Jesse Fisher's body had just been taken into the house when Manuel Garcia and Jose Perez rode up on horses. They claimed that they had been late with their chores and had not started the milking until about 8:00 P.M. They had just started when five men came into the barn and held them up. The men took them a distance from the barn and tied their hands. Three of the men left, leaving two masked men to guard them. Over an hour passed, then they heard shots from the direction of the ranch house. When this happened the guards disappeared into the darkness.

The two Mexicans said that they thought the ranch was being attacked by a band of raiders and with their hands tied, there were helpless. They ran a mile and a half to the home of William Hughes, a half-breed Mexican, who freed their hands and brought them back to the Slaughter ranch.

One part of the Mexican's story did not ring true. Between the time the shots were fired and the arrival of Perez, Garcia, and Hughes at the ranch, more than an hour had passed. They claimed that all of this time was consumed in going to and from

Hughes' house, saying that Hughes was in bed and that a half hour passed while he was getting dressed and untying their hands.

Percy Bowden, Billy Fourr, and John Lawton were present when the two Mexicans returned. Mrs. Slaughter said that she had seen two men jump out of the stone house into the streak of light that shone out of the window where Mr. Slaughter usually sat. (John's guardian angel was with him as he had, unexpectedly, gone into the bedroom.) Viola said that she had recognized Manuel Garcia just as he fired two shots from a revolver. She saw Fisher fall as she ran into the house.

Whoever shot Fisher walked up to the body, turned it over with his foot, and then went into the commissary where his bloody footprints were found on the floor. Bloody fingerprints were also on the door.

Fingerprints, which were developed and traced by Day Sergeant Murchison, an expert in this field, were found on the back of a check which had been in the commissary till. The killers had snatched it from the drawer and threw it on the floor thinking it valueless, leaving the imprint of the bloody fingers plainly visible. Garcia's prints matched those on the check perfectly.

The following day a coroner's jury delivered a verdict of "death due to gunshot wounds inflicted by known parties, to wit, Manuel Garcia and Jose Perez".

The two men were brought to trial the next September before Judge Alfred Lockwood. They were convicted as accessories in second degree murder and sentenced to life imprisonment in the state penitentiary at Florence.

It was soon revealed that neither of the two men that were convicted actually shot Jesse Fisher. two other men, who were involved in the murder and robbery, shot the hapless Fisher. They were Arcadio Chavez and Manuel Rubio.

About a month after the murder, Chavez was apprehended in Agua Prieta and confessed that he and Rubio had done the shooting, not Garcia and Perez. The latter two had been involved in the planning and execution of the robbery, but were innocent of the murder. Chavez said that he shot Fisher with a Mauser rifle and that Manuel Rubio fired the second shot into Fisher from a revolver. Chavez was found to have Fisher's watch in his possession and admitted that he took it from the dead body after the shooting. He also revealed that the bandits had planned to steal everything in sight and to kill everyone who attempted to prevent their purpose. That plan fell through when John Slaughter kept moving about in the house. They realized that any attempt to enter the house would result in his killing the first ones to enter.

Cochise County officials attempted to extradite Chavez but the effort was unsuccessful. Manuel Rubio was never captured. The Mexican government, reluctantly, moved the prisoner to Hermosillo, where he was tried and found guilty.

At that time Mexico and the United States had no treaty permitting the extradition of men accused of murder in either country. A kind of unwritten agreement existed along the border for handling red-handed murderers when caught in either country, by just overlooking the law in the crossing of criminals across the border to the country desiring them for heinous crimes.

Earlier in 1921, Governor Calles secured the persons of some men accused of the murder and robbery of Mexican customs officials between Agua Prieta and Cananea. These culprits were found in Douglas and were taken across the border at night by persons unknown. Early the next morning the three men were seen hanging by their necks from telephone poles within plain view of the Douglas streets. Naturally, this caused a furor in Washington and a number of investigations were initiated; however, no one was identified as being responsible for allowing these men to be summarily taken from this country.

Manuel Garcia was pardoned by the Governor of Arizona in 1929.

A few weeks after Fisher's murder, John and Viola left the ranch and moved into Douglas to the Fisher Apartments at

12th Street and E Avenue. John went back to the ranch to visit and to manage its affairs until the day before he died. Viola did not return to the ranch at all for fourteen years.

By the end of 1921, the old lawman suffered from eczema of the hands and feet and from high blood pressure. He made two trips to the Indian Hot Springs in Graham County, but that improved his health very little.

On February 15, 1922, John went out to the San Bernardino. When he returned that night he complained of a headache. A few days before he had seemed somewhat weaker. Dr. Greene came out to the ranch to check his headache that night. He stayed until John was sleeping quietly then left a little past midnight. Viola went into John's bedroom about five o'clock the next morning. The entire room was dark, quiet and still. During the wee hours of the morning John had saddled up old Gray and taken the out trail.

Thus the long and exciting life of John Horton Slaughter came to an end after over eighty years, just as he had always predicted. . .in bed, with his boots off.

John must have sensed that death was near, as just a few days before he had told Viola, "When I die, I do not wish to be buried in Tombstone, because Tombstone will soon be a ghost town and I want to be buried where there are people."

The funeral of John Horton Slaughter was one of the most impressive and largely attended affairs ever witnessed in Douglas. The number of prominent men, coming from all parts of the country, attested the widespread popularity of the deceased. It also showed the desire of those who had known Mr. Slaughter during the days of intense activity and usefulness to pay him a last tribute of honor and respect.

A great crowd overflowed the Episcopal Church on Eleventh Street and E Avenue, unable to gain admittance, as Reverend E.W. Simonson conducted the funeral services. The pallbearers were a roll call of John's best friends: C.A. Overlock, H.M. Wood, James H. East, John Grigbaum, Rafael Gabilondo, and George H. Kelley. The honorary pall bearers were more of the same: Hugh Conlin, William Lutley, B.A. Packard, H.C. Stillman, Judge Fletcher Doan, and Tim Taft.

Floral offerings were present in profusion and the casket was covered with beautiful roses. The flowers were considered to be the finest ever seen in Douglas. All of them were sent to the county hospital after the funeral.

After the church services the remains were removed to the front door of the church and the casket was opened to allow the crowd to take a last look at their old friend. The march to the cemetery extended in a column from Tenth Street to the cemetery. John was buried beside Willie.

The Tombstone Epitaph, February 19, 1922, carried the following article:

"JOHN SLAUGHTER PIONEER

The old west is going!
The west of which the poet sang:
'Out where the world is in the making.
Where fewer hearts in despair are aching.
That's where the west begins;
Where there's more of singing and less of sighing,
Where there's more of giving and less of buying
And a man makes friends without half trying-
That's where the west begins.'

"For John Slaughter, pioneer has passed like the ships that pass in the night. Cochise County's grand old man complained and slept and never wakened. And so passed one of the great characters of Arizona."

"John Slaughter is famed in song and story. His exploits have coursed round the globe. His friends have been legion and his enemies he has been proud of. His life has been full of work, of love and accomplishment."

"When Cochise was young as a political subdivision of a wild western territory, John Slaughter came to see. He drove his herd to the San Pedro and camped. He has been here ever since. In the meantime he has seen life; and life as it was lived in those strenuous days of the seventies and eighties.

"John Slaughter's record will live long in any history of this county. He is chiefly remembered as its sheriff. There are many sheriffs famed in song and fable. Most of them have gained their fame through the facility with which they used their trigger finger. John Slaughter, however, gained his fame as a staunch supporter of the law, by his ability to take trouble in its incipiency and prevent its consequences. Yet he did not fear man or devil. He shot straight, when shooting was necessary. He rarely missed his mark and the bandits and desperados of his day testified to his prowess."

"When John Slaughter was sheriff the law was a written thing. It had hardly found lodgement in the hearts of the people. But the new sheriff believed the law was to be enforced. He believed in the rights of property. He was firmly convinced that life was of value and should be protected. On that premise he reigned in Cochise and woe to the man who directed this scheme of ours otherwise. For John Slaughter never quit."

"As a builder, John Slaughter has accomplished much. The San Bernardino ranch will remain a monument to his faith, His hope for Arizona never faltered. He lived to see it grow and prosper."

"John Slaughter is dead, but the spirit of the old west, the better- part of the west that was, still lives in the memory of the present generation and the name of Slaughter will forever, in Cochise, stand synonymous for law enforcement. That heritage John Slaughter leaves his family, his friends, and his state."

Like many of those who won fame and respect while taming the west, John Slaughter would be totally unacceptable to the weak and shallow but politically and socially correct society of today. He did what was necessary to bring justice to the times. If that meant a horse thief or killer died without a trial or burial, or if a rancher was frightened out of the country ...well... Arizona Territory was no place for weaklings anyway.

The Out Trail

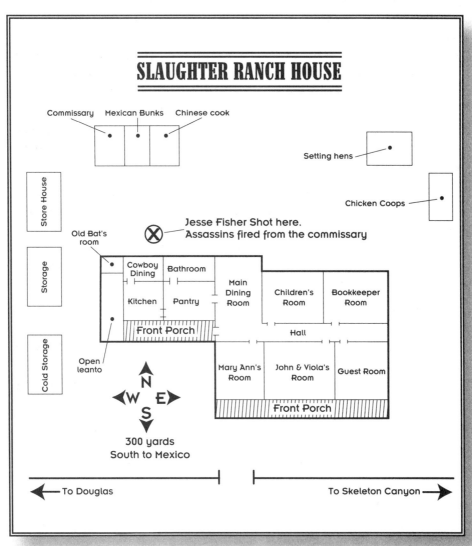

— The Slaughter ranch —

Viola Slaughter
1924

John Slaughter (center) — 1900

John Slaughter
Fishing

Viola Slaughter

Photos courtesy of Marge & Steve Elliott

John, Viola and friends

Photos courtesy of Marge & Steve Elliott

John, Viola and friends

Photos courtesy of Marge & Steve Elliott

> No. 64
>
> In the matter of the inquest held on the body of
>
> Year 1890
>
> David D. Duncan, Deceased.
>
> Inquest held by Rat Hawk, acting Coroner.
>
> PROCEEDINGS.
>
> Jan 27 — Inquest held.
> 30 — Filed:
>   Cause of death, a gunshot, and two knife wounds.

David D. Duncan
Inquest notice of death

> No. 225
>
> In the matter of the Inquest held on the body of
>
> Year 1890
>
> W. W. Louther, Deceased.
>
> Inquest held by S. C. Amin, J. P., acting Coroner.
>
> PROCEEDINGS.
>
> April 11 — Inquest held.
> May 12 — Filed
>   Cause of death, Gunshot wound. Deceased was a native of the State of Arkansas aged Forty five years.

W.W. Louther
Inquest notice of death

374	In the matter of the inquest held on the body of		Inquest held by	
1898	Arthur Finney Deceased.		S. V. Williams Coroner.	
		PROCEEDINGS.	Dr.	Cr.
Sept 20	Inquest held			
28	" Filed			
	Cause of death; from the effects of three gunshot wounds while resisting arrest by Dept. U.S. marshal J. H. Slaughter while in discharge of his duty.			

Arthur Finney
Inquest notice of death

— Death Certificate - Mary Ann Howell —
Died of Influenza/pneumonia on April 9, 1920

That Wicked Little Gringo

— Death Certificate - Jesse H. Fisher —
Died of gun shot wounds on May 4, 1921

Fisher Apartments — 12th & E Avenue, Douglas
*The Slaughters lived here after leaving the ranch.
John died at this location.*

**Viola lived in this house on 9th Street in
Douglas after John's death.**

— Death Certificate - John Swain —
Died of myocarditis degenerative on February 8, 1945

In the Justice Court

Fourth Precinct, County of Cochise, State of Arizona

#1449

In the matter of inquisition into the Cause of Death of

Jesse Fisher
(Deceased)

VERDICT OF CORONER'S JURY.

STATE OF ARIZONA,
County of Cochise } ss.

We the undersigned, having been summoned and sworn by **Wm. G. Jack**, a coroner of **Cochise** County, State of Arizona, to act as jurors in the matter of the inquisition into the cause of the death of **Jesse Fisher**, having viewed the remains and having heard and considered all the evidence presented, and being duly informed in the premises, upon our oaths do say: that from the evidence adduced, we do find the facts to be as follows:

That the name of the deceased was **Jesse Fisher** and that he was of the age of about **58** years at the time of death; that he came to **his** death in or near the City or Town of **Douglas**, County of **Cochise**, State of Arizona, at about the hour of **9** o'clock, P.M., on the **4th** day of **May**, 19**21** from (cause of death) **gun shot wounds at the hands of parties unknown**

~~[struck through text]~~

to-wit: — Manuel Garcia
Jose Perez

In all of which we certify by attaching our signatures hereto, it is **6th** day of **May**, 19**21**.

Witnesses.
Dr. W. A. Greene
Mrs. J. H. Slaughter
Miss Stone

C. P. Harvey
Jack Baumbeck
Garland Coffey
Ed Furlong
W. F. Kahoran
H. E. Conlon
Wm Jack

Coroner. Fourth Precinct, Cochise County, Arizona

Jesse Fisher Death — Verdict of Coroner's Jury
*Finding: Jessee died at the hand of others,
to wit: Manual Garcia and Jose Perez.*

Sources:

Douglas Daily Dispatch, November 9, 1906
    Ibid, ... October 24, 1907
    Ibid, ... May 5, 1921
    Ibid, ... May 6, 1921
    Ibid, ... May 7, 1921
    Ibid, ... May 8, 1921
    Ibid, ... May 9, 1921
    Ibid, ... May 15, 1921
    Ibid, ... February 16, 1922
    Ibid, ... February 19, 1922
Douglas International . . . . . . February 20, 1922
Douglas Daily Dispatch . . . . . February 21, 1922
    Ibid, ... April 3, 1941
    Ibid, ... April 4, 1941
Tombstone Epitaph. . . . . May 15, 1921
    Ibid, ... February 19, 1922

Ben T. Traywick
presents

Greetings from Tombstone, A.T. 1/14/02
Ben T. Traywick

That
WICKED LITTLE GRINGO

(Story of Tombstone's John Slaughter)

Published by **RED MARIE'S BOOKSTORE**
P.O. Box 891 Tombstone, Arizona

That Wicked Little Gringo
(Story of Tombstone's John Slaughter)
by
Ben T. Traywick

Published 2001 Red Marie's Books
Tombstone, Arizona
©2001 by Ben T. Traywick

This one is for Mary Dolores

Cover Artwork from a painting by Mike James
Cover Layout by Lee Baker